Joy Dance

52 Joy-votions that Free your Heart to Grow in Jesus

Robbie Iobst

All Scripture References are from the New International Version
unless otherwise stipulated.

ISBN: 0-6157-0630-4
ISBN-13: 9780615706306

Dedication:

For John and Noah, my daily joys.

CONTENTS

Section 1–JOY IN HIS PRESENCE

1 A Light Bulb of Faith   3

2 Soul Rest   5

3 The Good Physician's Grace   7

4 Crave His Presence   9

5 One Thing   11

6 Pay Attention   13

7 Head to the Closet   15

8 Love Letter   17

9 Look Around and Cheer–Go God!   19

10 Today, It's on Him   21

11 Who Are You?   23

12 Lunch Box Dreams   25

13 God is For You!   27

Section 2–JOY IN GROWTH

14 Bone Tired   31

15 Soul Satisfying   33

16 Let It Go   35

17 We Need Elbows   37

18 Anyone Have an Abacus?   39

19 Saying No to Bunny Sandwiches   41

20 Let Him Paint   43

21 Page 430   47

22 May I Have Some More-Ish?   51

23 We All Need His Flashlight   53

24 See You at the Finish   55

25 Turn North   57

26 Declare Your Independence from Fear   59

Section 3–JOY IN THE BATTLE

27 Can I Borrow a Cup of Sugar?   65

28 Never Alone   67

29 Who Do You Trust?   69

30 Lightning Beats Flames Every Time   71

31 Hang On!   73

32 Valleys   75

33 Remember   77

34 He is For You   81

35 No Black Dress For Me   85

36 Living in a Might Situation   87

37 Turn the Page   89

38 You'll Need a Tent Peg and a Hammer   91

39 Remember Who You Are   93

Section 4–JOY IN FAMILY

40 Mad Skills   97

41 He See the Broken Windows   99

42 Can You Spell Pain?   101

43 The Joy of a Dog   103

44 Ding! It's Ready!   105

45 Family–Take it up with God   107

46 You Got Him, God?   109

47 Get Out of God's Way   113

48 Maybe, Maybe Not   115

49 Discount Dog Gamble   117

50 I'm a Horrible Mother   119

51 Stick the Landing   121

52 When Fear Rings Your Door Bell   123

Acknowledgments:

Thank you Jesus for giving me an abundant life! Thank you John, Marriah, Sarah, Hannah and Noah for adding FAMILY to my life. Thank you Loretta Oakes, Kay Day, Michele Cushatt, Stacy Voss and Dianne Daniels for being wonderful friends and critique partners. Thank you Sharen Watson for mentoring me, Megan DiMaria for encouraging and guiding me and Denise Holmes for teaching me through *Words for the Journey Christian Writers Guild*. Thanks to all the wonderful writers and friends who've cheered me on. Thank you Karen Pratt, Lory Floyd and Kasey Floyd for being my sisters and prayer warriors. A special note of gratitude to my husband John for writing two of these Joyvotions - #11 "Who Are You" and #48 "Maybe, Maybe Not." And thank you so much to each of you who have read my weekly Joyvotions and encouraged me to keep scribbling. To God be the glory!

Prologue:

Joy is not just a feeling of giddiness. In God's kingdom, joy is knowing God is in control and we are in His hands no matter the circumstances. It's a choice to rest in Him.

This book contains 52 of the weekly Joy-votions I wrote over the past four years. They are not in chronological order; instead I grouped them together in four sections: Joy in His Presence, Joy in Growth, Joy in the Battle and Joy in Family. My goal in writing these and putting this book together is to inspire you to laugh, relax and rest in who you are and who HE IS. Psalm 16:11 says "In His presence is fullness of joy..." Joy is not about how we act or feel. It is simply a reaction to the One who adores us.

My hope and prayer is that after you read a Joyvotion, you will look up to Jesus and open your heart to a little bit more of His presence, His love and yep, His JOY! Wouldn't it be sweet to live life as a Joy Dance, following His lead?

One
Joy in His Presence

1 A Light Bulb of Faith

"And without faith it is impossible to please God,
because anyone who comes to him must believe
that he exists and that he rewards those who earnestly seek him."
Hebrews 11:4

Noah, my nine-year-old son, walked into the kitchen, obviously ready to make an announcement.

"Mom, I've decided."

"What?"

"For Christmas, I want…" Noah jumped into a detailed description of a certain Lego's set, complete with specific name, color and possible asking price.

I *actually knew* what he was talking about. "Noah, they discontinued that set. Lego doesn't make it anymore."

Dejected and forlorn, my boy stared at me. I must have made a mistake. "Are you sure?"

"Yes, I'm certain."

Noah took a moment and contemplated his life, a sad pathetic existence. What was the point of being alive without the Lego set he desired? But then…

A light came into his eyes. I almost saw the light bulb appear above his head. "Santa can make them at the North Pole! I'm sure of it!" He promptly left the kitchen. The matter had been settled.

Such belief. Pure. Simple. A child-like faith.

My boy's unwavering loyalty to Santa inspires me. Do I have the same degree of belief in God? The God of Abraham? The Father, the Son and the Holy Spirit? I hope I do.

Without faith it is impossible to please God. I first must believe that HE IS and that HE rewards me when I seek HIM.

It starts with belief. It starts with faith.

Ten days ago, my husband was involved in a motorcycle accident that left him in an ICU with a traumatic head injury. The moment I received news of his crash, I was presented with a choice, the same one I would battle daily. Robbie, do you believe that:

a) God is in control? Or

b) Fate, medical science and cause and effect are calling the shots?

A choice. If God is truly in control, fear is not needed. The perfect love of Christ eliminates the fear that seeks to dwell and consume.

But if my husband was the victim of a random, Russian-roulette incident, then fear would naturally be my constant companion.

I chose God. Not without doubt. Faith without doubt is blind devotion. I ain't blind! But I know that God is real, and that He rewards those who seek Him. He could've rewarded me with strength to see through a funeral and dark grief and loneliness as a single mom. He could've rewarded me with the joy, deep abiding joy of His presence even as I buried my best friend and soul mate.

But He didn't. Instead He rewarded me with an army of prayer warriors, all over the country, willing to go to God for John. He rewarded me with miraculous progress for John in the ICU. He rewarded me with a precious moment in which I saw my husband, my John, come back to me.

Now, as John battles recovery at a rehab facility, God continues to reward us with the mending of relationships in our family and the rediscovered joy of old friendships.

God is not like Santa, up there with a nice and naughty list, waiting to dole out gifts or coal. God is unexplainable and indefinable. He is bigger than anything I can ever imagine. But HE IS!

And today I believe. I choose to practice my faith and sit back and watch what He will do next.

When doubt comes, I take a moment and contemplate my life. What would the point of my life be without His goodness and comfort and joy?

A light comes into my heart and the light bulb of faith once again appears.

God can do whatever He wants. He loves me and He will help me. I'm sure of it!

2 Soul Rest

"Be at rest once more, o my soul,
for the Lord has been good to you."
Psalm 116:7

"He restores my soul."
Psalm 23:3

Women crying on soap operas make me sick.

No blotchy skin, no runny mascara. Just faultless faces and perfectly shaped tears falling gently down one cheek.

Gag. When I cry, I resemble a mix between a nuclear blowfish and Louie Armstrong. Plus there's all the snot. It's not pretty.

Since my husband's motorcycle accident, my tears have scared small children, worried old ladies and caused an avalanche of advice from well meaning friends.

"Robbie, you must get some rest. You've been through a lot."

So I've tried. My father taught me how to breathe deeply before sleep. The art is to make tiny little tunnels of air. Slowly inhale through the nose and concentrate on exhaling tiny tunnels as you exhale. For the most part, it's worked ever since.

But not lately. Sleep comes eventually, but not soul rest. So I've tried other things, like long baths, walks under the magnificent Colorado sky, a pajama day. Even a trip to Hobby Lobby, my first, to find a cathartic craft.

Great experiences. But none brought rest. Inner, deep soul rest.

So, and I am not proud to admit this, I turned to the Bible as a last resort. Now don't get me wrong, I love reading Scripture and I try to every day. But as I opened it this time, it was for one purpose. To find rest. I tried a little experiment to see if God's Words could really rest my soul. Restore me.

I read verse after verse, slowly. Sometimes repeating passages. Between the verses, I used my dad's method and created those tiny tunnels. And I felt it. Something small and familiar and yet new. It was as if someone was massaging my heart.

I'm still tired. I still cry. Yesterday I bawled like a baby in the lobby of a church. A friend wanted to know what was wrong. Noah stood near me as I said, "I just need to cry." And then to Noah I said, "Do I cry a lot these days, Noah?" With a hint of a grin he looked at my friend. "A lot."

I'm not there yet. But I'm on my way to rest – oration. I am.

Most of us lead exhausting lives, don't we? You may not be as emotional as I am, but the craving for rest in today's world is common. Not a power nap. Real soul rest. God has a craving, too. He wants to draw us in and give us what we need. Try my experiment. Instead of an evening of TV or sleeping in, ingest the Word of God. Enter into His rest. And don't forget the tiny tunnels.

3 The Good Physician's Grace

"Grace be unto you, and peace, from God our Father,
and from the Lord Jesus Christ."
Philippians 2:1

For the past seven days, with the exception of Sunday, John has been in a hospital, doctor's office or had home health care. Most of the time I was by his side.

So I've thought a lot lately about physicians, surgeons and nurses. Each is an individual with his/her own family, problems and joys. Each is cherished by God.

However, John and I have found it difficult to cherish these wonderful souls. We've said, "Thank you." We've been polite. But we've also made sarcastic comments to one another, under our breath. We've growled, little guttural mutterings, loosely translated as "CAN YOU BELIEVE THIS??!!"

And we've laughed. We had to. Two grown people bawling in a doctor's office is a bit pathetic. Even for the Iobst clan.

But a couple of moments have been so absurd, we've shed tears while laughing.

Once, the wound doctor used a big 'ole scary needle to suck out 10 ccs of John's blood clot under his wound. I've never seen John in such horrific pain.

Right after, a nurse using a monotone voice, said, "Was your pain sharp, dull or throbbing?"

John and I glanced at each other and burst out laughing.

He replied through tears, "How about screaming like a little girl?"

It would be so nice if we could just go to the Good Physician's office and let him heal the leg wound, bless it and then we'd leave.

But God doesn't work that way. Not always. He uses imperfect people and an imperfect medical community to do His job. The process of going through all of this is part of His healing plan.

Two home health care nurses just left our condo. When they came and curiously eyed the wound vac equipment shipped to our home, I asked, "Have you ever done a wound vac before?"

Silence. Then one said, "Not many." And she picked up the user's manual and began reading the installation instructions.

Once again John and I exchanged glances. Two guttural noises arose. And then we laughed. About the time we quieted down, one of the nurses in an Alabama accent casually said, "Boy, they sure do have a lot of gadgets in this."

While tears ran down my laughing face, I silently prayed, "Good Physician, please help!"

John spoke aloud. "That's the least comforting thing I've ever heard anyone say."

After three hours and two tries, they succeeded.

I wonder what God thinks about situations like this. Maybe He giggles with us and whisper, "Don't worry." Or does He cringe and say, "You've got to be kidding me?"

I think neither. I think the Good Physician held each of us – John, me and those two nurses – each of us at our point of need and quietly doctored with love and grace.

4 Crave His Presence

"Haven't I commanded you? Strength! Courage! Don't be timid; don't get discouraged. God, your God, is with you every step you take."
Joshua 1:9
"The distance all around will be 18,000 cubits. and the name of the city from that time on will be The LORD is There." Ezekiel 48:35
Jehovah Shammah – The LORD is there

Do you smell that? It's the unmistakable scent of turkey being sliced and hot pumpkin pies. It's the perfume of joy and expectation. It's the odor of greed and anxiety.

It's the holidays.

For the next six weeks, many of us will be planning, shopping, visiting and eating more than usual. The culture of America dictates that the last half of November and all of December are to be happy and busy. This is a lie. See, this is also the time of year when people are the saddest and the loneliest.

When Christ was born He was given the name Emmanuel meaning God with Us. Why is it at Christmas many of us forget that He is with us? Instead, we concentrate on the menus and the lists of presents.

In Ezekiel, the author describes Jerusalem and the temple. When Christ returns to gather His people, Ezekiel tells us the name of Jerusalem will be changed to Jehovah Shammah – The LORD is There.

But as I studied this name, I found out that although Jehovah Shammah represents completion, it also means The LORD is Present. Now.

He's right here. I have a tremendous imagination, so early in my walk with Christ I would imagine Him with me. He stood in the back of the classroom when I taught, cheering me on. He held me up when I watched my mother die. He drove around and car-danced with me.

Some may call this practice silly. I call it faith.

As I type this, I am sitting at Starbucks enjoying a Tazo Joy hot tea. And Christ is with me, whispering ideas for this Joyvotion.

In Exodus 33:15 Moses says, "If your Presence does not go with us, do not send us up from here." As the Israelites began the journey into the wilderness, Moses couldn't bear the thought of going without the presence of God.

Today I encourage you and me to look at the next six weeks like a wilderness, full of malls and family and parties. Or maybe for you it is a wilderness full of regret or loneliness or anger.

Whatever your circumstance, crave the Lord's presence like Moses did.

Jehovah Shammah is with you. While you read this, look up and imagine Christ near you. Try it, I dare you.

In your step of faith, God will reward you. He will. He'll give you the best gift of all: His presence.

5 One Thing

"Come aside by yourselves to a deserted place and rest a while."
Mark 6:31

Have you been alone with Christ this week? By that, I mean have you focused on God when no one else was around?

If not, then let me put it simply: *You are missing out.*

We get so busy with our lists of to-dos we forget to take time for the One who gives us guidance and strength to accomplish the to-do lists.

I've known Jesus since I was a young girl. My relationship with Him has had its ups and downs. I've ignored Him and adored Him. I've run to Him and away from Him. He's let circumstances brought on by my actions humble me, sometimes painfully.

However, in the last five years my relationship with Jesus has changed dramatically. It's deeper and richer and much more rewarding. Why?

It's NOT because:

1) We joined a new church.
2) We moved to Colorado.
3) I joined a Bible Study.
4) I started writing Joyvotions.
5) I began speaking regularly.
6) John's accident, the joys and trials of Noah or Scooby, my faithful dog.
7) Good or bad times in our marriage.
8) I have wonderful Christian friends.

So why has my relationship changed? It is because of ONE thing.

Time alone with my King

What used to be a quiet time of reading and praying has now become a lifestyle of making a PRIORITY to be with Jesus alone for an extended period of time. I regularly make an appointment to sit at Christ's feet and listen to Him. Sometimes it's for an afternoon; sometimes a day and sometimes I go to a cabin at a retreat center and seclude myself with Christ for a weekend.

(These are called WAAWGs – Weekends almost alone with God – a habit/behavior I learned from my brother Phil and his ministry Caleb's Heart – www.calebsheart.com)

It's changed me. And why wouldn't it? If we put aside the phone, internet, TV and people and hang out with God, of course, we will be changed for the better.

I encourage you to do this. Make time. If you have no idea how to go about this, email me and I'll give you the hints I've learned.

You want more from your life? Spend time alone with the King.

6 Pay Attention

"As the deer pants for the water brooks,
So pants my soul for You, O God."
Psalm 42:1

Have you ever been hot and thirsty? When you really want water? I think we all have experienced this at one time or another. This morning Scooby and I walked hard uphill and when we came home the first thing both of us did was go to the kitchen. I for my water bottle and Scooby for his water bowl.

I live in a physical body and I need water to live. My soul, on the other hand, needs the living water of Jesus Christ. Each of us was made to have a relationship with Him. Our souls crave it.

It is amazing how God has put cravings within each of us that can only be filled by living for Him. I'm not just talking about conviction we might feel or desperation for His help. But what about those moments when our insides light up with longing for joy and the gifts that bring us joy?

When I look at my husband and he gives me that grin reserved for me, my soul smiles. Is that moment related to God? Yes! It is my Creator that has put John and me together. And when I feel a sweet love toward my husband, it is a signal that God loves me and is drawing me to Him through the marriage I have.

When I hear a tennis ball bouncing on a court, I get a twinge of joy. I played tennis as a child and teenager and loved it. I don't play very often anymore, but when I do, I sense His presence. That twinge is a longing to experience the joy of running across a court and using a backhand swing to cram the ball over the net and into the corner where my opponent is not. Is this related to God? Yes! God gave me the ability to play and love tennis. A longing for the tennis court is a longing to use the gifts God gave me.

When I sit at my laptop and an idea comes for writing, it is a highly spiritual moment of connecting with the One who made me to be a writer. Of course, this is related to God. As I use that idea and feel my fingers fly over the keyboard, I am longing for the Author of all to write through me.

Are you panting for God and looking to Him to quench your thirst for meaning? It is too easy to forget God and experience moments like I've just listed and miss the connection to the Father in daily experiences. One of the greatest practices you and I can do to live closely to Jesus each day is to PAY ATTENTION. Watch for God at work in you. It's not only in moments at church or when you're praying. He made us. He made us to be in relationship, to enjoy the simple moments like lobbing a tennis ball up high and getting ready in case the return comes fast. And He made us to find work that we love so He can use those abilities to minister through us and to us.

As the deer walks up to a stream, panting and looking for his "water bottle," so you and I can go through each day longing for His presence in everything we do. Pay attention and savor the Living Water of life.

7 Head to the Closet

"But I will sing of your strength, in the morning I will sing of your love;
for you are my fortress, my refuge in times of trouble."
Psalm 59:16

This morning I was driving to meet a friend while KLOVE, the Christian radio station, was on in my car. A woman called in and told the story of a youth pastor she knows who lives in Joplin. When the tornado hit last week, he was not at home, but his wife and toddler were. When the twister descended, the youth pastor's wife took her little one and went into a closet. She prayed with her child and sang a hymn loudly to fight the fear.

When the tornado ended, the wife opened up the closet and discovered that her entire home was gone. **Everything except the closet.**

God is at work.

I started thinking about that closet. Just a small place to hold clothes. But God used it miraculously in the life of that family. The closet became the refuge, the protection against the storm.

I am not in the midst of a crisis. Denver has blue skies and warm weather today. It's gorgeous. No storms on the horizon.

But yet, I know the closet is there for me. He is a refuge for me *every day.*

This past week I've had a nasty cold. Trivial, yes. But what I do with that miniscule problem is huge in how I relate to God. And it's practice for the storms that come.

So what are my choices?

a)   Whine.
b)   Exhaust myself trying to take care of everybody else, even though I'm sick.
c)   Rest.

d)   Find my closet.

The answer is d. Go into my closet and snuggle up to Him. Talk. Sing a hymn. Loudly.

If I do that now, then when something major hits, my immediate reaction will be head to the closet.

When your kids are sick and you feel helpless, head to the closet.

When you have more bills than money, head to the closet.

When you or someone you love is stuck in an addiction, head to the closet.

When you want to forgive, but just can't, head to the closet.

When you have a nasty cold, head to the closet.

He will meet you there. Your world may collide but our Father in heaven, our refuge every moment of every day, will not leave you.

We never know when a tornado will hit and it could be a twister that takes away precious parts of our lives.

Except the closet. God will always be there.

8 Love Letter

"Since you are precious and honored in my sight,
and because I love you..."
Isaiah 43:4

Dear Child,

I love you.

I love you with an everlasting, never-ending, no-matter-what-happens love. (Jeremiah 31:3)

I love you even if you: yell at your kids, lie, cheat on your taxes, speed down the freeway, ignore Me or put yourself down.

I love you no matter what. (Psalm 66:20)

I love you when: You are exhausted and feel sorry for yourself. You are exhausted and have a great attitude. You are grieving. You are laughing. You are sinning. (Psalm 86:5 and 86:13)

I love you if: *there is no if.*

You can know I love you because:
- I sent Jesus to die for you so we could have a forever relationship. (John 3:16)
- I say it in My Word. (Isaiah 43:4)
- I pour My love into you through the Holy Spirit. (Romans 5:5)
- I don't let anything separate you and My love. (Romans 8: 35-39)
- I am love. (1 John 4:8)

I love you!

This Valentine's Week you may get roses or not, or a card or not, or a date or not. You may hate the day because you are lonely or because you don't like the one you're with. You may love every minute of this week because you are a romantic or because you are blissfully in love.

How you see this week is how you see it.

But what I care about is your heart that I adore. (Ezekiel 36:26)

I cherish you.

In fact, *I delight in you!* (Zephaniah 3:17) (Psalm 18:19)

I love you!

Just wanted you to know.

The relentless pursuer of your heart,

God

9 Look Around And Cheer – Go God!

"You will go out in joy and be led forth in peace; the mountains and hills will burst into song before you, and all the trees of the field will clap their hands." Isaiah 55:12
"Blessed is the king who comes in the name of the Lord!
Peace in heaven and glory in the highest!"
Some of the Pharisees in the crowd said to Jesus,
"Teacher, rebuke your disciples!"
"I tell you," he replied, "if they keep quiet, the stones will cry out."
Luke 19:38-40

Three rows ahead and to the left. That's where he sat with his grandson. During worship, he stood holding onto his grandson with one arm, while the other arm rose with a hand lifted up, surrendering to the Father. When he sang, his lips moved ever so slightly, but I could tell every word meant something.

God's beauty comes in all forms. This past week, I've been overwhelmed by it. For example:

My stepdaughter Sarah posted a picture on Facebook of my granddaughter Lucy Ophelia on Easter. She's hundreds of miles away, and in that moment I felt her on my lap with her smooth nine-month-old skin and sweet smile that communicates the innocence of childhood right along with the gorgeous love of God.

I went to the Botanic Gardens with some of my Bible Study friends. I couldn't believe the different colors and types of tulips! From flowers that looked like Dr. Seuss drew them, to a purple cactus with yellow buds, the garden displays the creativity, the wonder of God.

At a movie theatre on Friday night, I sat with a group of friends and family and watched Donald Miller's *Blue Like Jazz*. Several times I heard my brother Phil's full throated raucous laugh that is born of a belly full of Jesus. Beautiful.

John, Noah and I attended a concert in which the Denver Concert band played an eclectic range of songs, including "Blue and Green Music" by Samuel R. Hazo. That song whisked me away and I imagined myself in heaven, dancing and flying with Christ, my own personal soundtrack in the background.

And finally, the grandfather in church. His white, thin hair reminded me of an old eagle's feathers. A tuft of it stuck straight up at the top of his forehead. Wire glasses sat low on his nose and the wrinkles on his face told so many stories. Stories I'll never know. But after watching this beautiful old man worship in church, I know every story was worth it. Each a puzzle piece in a portrait of God's beauty.

We get busy and forget to look around at the beauty that God has for us. Yesterday I ate two of the best fish tacos I've ever eaten at the California Pizza Kitchen here in Denver. Go God! As I write this I'm listening to "Forever" a secular pop song by Chris Brown. It may not have been written to glorify the Father, but the joy in the music is originated in our God and in His beauty!

Look around! Taste His goodness and hear His joy. Watch for the splendor of the Father in the faces around you. We may not glorify God in all our choices, but His creations cannot help glorifying Him. Praise His Name for His beauty!

10 Today, It's On Him!

"I have loved you with an everlasting love;
I have drawn you with unfailing kindness will I draw you to me."
Jeremiah 31:3

"Robbie, let me treat you." Five of my favorite words!

Don't you just love it when you are having coffee with someone and they say that? And what a kick it is to be the one surprising your friend. It's not a huge thing, but the moment always brings me a smile and a little warm-up to the heart just as satisfying as morning coffee.

The other day, a friend of mine surprised me by treating me to a cup of hot ginger peach tea. As I sat to drink it, I felt the Spirit in me whisper, "I am FOR you, Robbie." It was as if God treated me to the tea, through my friend.

God wants to treat you and me. He is FOR us and He adores us. Last week I was in a three day funk, surrounded by negative thoughts and a pity party. God treated me to moments of hope and gave me a hand out of the pit I dug for myself.

TODAY, why don't you and I allow God to treat us? Watch what happens and see that He loves you, no matter your circumstances or your emotional state. He is FOR you! This morning God put the following words in my heart. For me and I hope and pray, for you.

Let Him Treat You
To a Taste of His Goodness,
To a Cup of Joy.
Let Him Treat You

To Peace during Anxiety,
To a Breath of Life during Smothering Pain.
Let Him Treat You
With Tenderness 'cause you are Worth it.
With Gentle Humor 'cause He Loves your Laugh.

Let Him Treat You
As Who You Are,
As Who You're Meant to Be,
As Who You're Becoming.
Let Him Treat You with His Infinite, Unconditional and Unrelenting
LOVE.

Today, God's buying!

11 Who Are You?

"And God said; Let us make man in our image, after our likeness: and let them have dominion over the fish of the sea, and over the fowl of the air, and over the cattle, and over all the earth, and over every creeping thing that creepeth upon the earth." Genesis 1:26

I went to a writer's conference a month or so ago and as John dropped me off at the airport, he said to me, "Robbie, no one gets to tell you your identity. No editor, no publisher, not another writer. Only God gets to speak to who you are."

His words had a profound effect on me. The following is written by my beloved husband John.

As a believer, I accept that God is my creator and by faith I have chosen to submit to Him as my Lord and King.

I drive a car that was "created" by Ford. They had a purpose in mind when they made this car. I can choose to load it up like a truck and I may have some success getting the load from point A to point B, but if I need a truck I should get a truck not a car. The purpose of anything is limited to the design and the design is defined by the designer. A boat is for sailing and a plane is for flying and with very few exceptions the two can't switch roles.

We humans all have many similarities in design (two legs, one head, opposable thumbs, etc.) so at some level we are all designed by our maker to fulfill the same purpose. But God gave us souls and free will so unlike animals, we can live beyond mere instinct and live out a very diverse and unique purpose.

So who gets to decide your purpose? I would argue that it is as simple as my car. The creator defines purpose. Additionally, I am convinced that purpose comes from identity so to know and live out your purpose you must know who you are.

The Rock Band "The Who" asked the question, "Who are you? Who, who, who, who?" We all struggle with that question and we often feel like we have failed to live up to what we were supposed to be. We feel that if anyone knew the truth about us, they would reject us.

So now we get to the real question. **Who gets to tell you your identity?** Should you listen to your boss when he/she gives you a rating on your work? What about a family member who decides to tell you your faults? Maybe you have a dream, and a friend tells you their opinion of your chances of achieving that dream. Allowing others to speak into your life can be valuable, but only if you let GOD speak first to your identity and your purpose.

Stop taking this question to other people or things. Instead, take it to your Creator who knew you while you were in your mother's womb. In the Bible, sometimes God gives new names. Jacob became Israel, Simon became Peter, James and John were known as the Sons of Thunder (talk about a very cool name.)

I believe God knows our real name and identity and will tell us if we ask. We often say "God has a plan for your life" and I am convinced that plan for each of us is rooted in our real name and identity that only God knows.

How to ask? Take time to be alone with God. No phone or distractions just time with the God who loves you and longs to set you free to be the real you He had in mind when He created you. When you discover your identity, remind yourself often of who He made you to be. So when the world tries to speak identity and purpose to you, you know the truth. You know who you are.

12 Lunch Box Dreams

"Jesus looked at them and said, "With man this is impossible, but not with God; all things are possible with God." Mark 10:27

When is the last time you sat by yourself and just dreamed? Or how about sitting with a close friend and dream aloud? No holds barred, no barriers or boundaries – you just let your mind and spirit go and race toward seeing your heart's desire fulfilled.

It's not an exercise for every day. Sloths dream and never work. But too many of us work and never dream. Really dream!

I was working at a Christian high school, sitting in a chapel service about ten or so years ago. Our principal, the great Chapin Marsh, talked to the students and teachers about POW – Possibilities, Opportunities and Why Not!!

The Lord who has chased me all my life with his unending love nudged me. I began to dream. Really dream.

Ten or so years later, I am living out what I dreamed that day. I am a writer and a speaker for Christ. It still amazes me. The dream came true through prayer and a lot of hard work. HOURS of sitting in a chair, staring at an empty screen and asking the Father to fill it up. He has. He continues to do so.

And the incredible fact of my life as I sit here pecking away at my laptop is the Lord who has chased me all my life with His unending love is not finished nudging me. I still dream! Really dream.

Of course, the road is full of obstacles and moments of "Why am I doing this?" and "I cannot write worth beans!" As you who have been faithful readers of my Joyvotions know, I have sunk to despair at times while eating gallons of ice cream.

But this Lord, this GREAT GOD of ours, just keeps loving me and nudging me to keep going. Keep dreaming.

God can do anything!! He fed 5000 folks with a kid's lunchbox! He is the God of the impossible.

I understand that I am not a famous writer. I haven't even published a book all of my own. YET. But the moments that I get to fulfill a tiny wish a high school teacher had years ago is JOY. Complete Joy!

I am so grateful to God for the moments I get to dream and the moments I get to live out my dream. I encourage you, faithful and wonderful reader of my scribbling, DREAM!! Take some time and just sit and say, "Okay God! You and me. Possibilities, Opportunities, Why Not? Lead me!"

He might just have a kid's lunchbox in His hands with YOUR NAME on it!

13 God Is For You!

"And the God of all grace, who called you to His eternal glory in Christ,
after you have suffered a little while,
will Himself restore you and make you strong, firm and steadfast."
1 Peter 5: 10

Today I am thankful for teeth that don't hurt. On Tuesday, I endured four hours in a dentist's chair. Two root canals and two cavity fillings later, I went home and promptly took some pain pills. Yesterday I continued taking my Vicodin and decided to put off writing a Joyvotion until today. My writing on Vicodin might be more entertaining, but I don't know if God would get any glory whatsoever.

I sit at Panera to write this while eating a cup of steak chili. I am so grateful to have teeth that are strong, firm and steadfast in order to enjoy my lunch. And at the risk of sounding incredibly cheesy but clever, I hope that my life is strong, firm and steadfast. (Great segue, right? I promise I'm not on any drugs.)

I am a big fan of 1 Peter 5:10. Most mornings as I walk, I recite this verse aloud. It reassures me that God is a God of all grace. **He's for me.** He's not out to get me. In fact, Isaiah tells us in Isaiah 30:18 that God longs to be gracious to us. He rises up to show us compassion. We each need that grace and compassion, don't we?

1 Peter 5:10 also delivers a little bit of reality to my life. "After you have suffered a little while..." It doesn't say IF, it says AFTER YOU HAVE suffered. Suffering is a part of life. Period. Accepting this fact saves so much trouble and energy running to other things so we don't have to feel pain. We are going to feel pain, folks. No way around it.

But then what? God Himself restores. He doesn't just leave us hanging with no hope. He comes and rescues us, not from pain, but from hopelessness that pain often brings.

And then the best part: God will "make you strong, firm and steadfast." This is after the suffering part. No suffering - no strong, firm and steadfast.

This brings me such hope and inspires me to persevere. As I sat in that dentist's chair, I prayed "GOD ARE YOU HERE?" I had to shout my prayer in my mind, because all I could hear was the cacophony of the chainsaw the dentist was using to carve open a tooth. God usually answers me in a still, quiet voice but He saw my situation and shouted back, "I'M HERE!"

Jehovah Shammah (The LORD is here) gave me hope and strength. And today my character is stronger, not just my steak-chewing teeth.

Before my root canals, the dentist prescribed me one valium to take before I came. When I went to the pharmacy, I discovered 10 pills in the bottle. So now, I have nine extra. Since holidays are coming and that means extended family, I am considering giving the valium as little gifts with notes attached saying, "To enjoy before the in-laws descend." It's my way of encouraging each of us to be strong, firm and steadfast.

I'm kidding, of course. But I so hope you look to Him for your hope and your strength. The God of all grace is for you.

Two
Joy in Growth

14 Bone Tired

"Be still and know that I am God."
Psalm 46:10

Bone tired. I like that phrase. Makes me think that the exhaustion goes past skin, blood and muscles all the way down to the bones. Yep, it fits.

I am exhausted as I write this. Just one of those weeks. Lots to do and many responsibilities.

But it is also Spring Break for my son. That means I have the privilege of spending extra time with the boy. I like that. We are enjoying our Spring Break chess tournament. We play once a day for nine days. Right now the score is 3-2. He's winning, but I will come back!

It means Lego building and extra snacks and movies. And today it meant watching he and four other boys go to an indoor pool and swim for hours. I love this time. I do.

But I am bushed.

After the pool party, we went to Chucky Cheese (we call him Pizza Rat) and Noah played games for an hour with all these extra tokens he's amassed. I played a bit with him, but when he sat down at the Star Wars Video Game, I went to a nearby table and rested.

And that's when I heard God's voice. Really quiet. Really beautiful.

"Be still, Robbie, and know that I am God."

I giggled because I happened to be sitting in one of the loudest places on earth. If you've had the honor of accompanying a child to this establishment, you understand this. Rock concerts don't have much on Chucky Cheese.

But again, God whispered, "Robbie be still. Know that I am God."

I took a deep breath and in this little booth I worshipped. I had a thanksgiving party for having such a great kid. I let God fill me up with His love and His strength.

Hours later I am bone tired. But because I took a little while and let God be God in my life, I am also spirit strong. It's a supernatural miracle that God can allow our physical bodies be weak and run down, and yet fill us to the brim with His vigorous strength.

Are you bone tired or on your way there? Take a moment and be still. Know that He is God. He yearns to fill you up with Spirit strength.

15 Soul Satisfying

"I will praise You as long as I live,
And in Your name I will lift up my hands.
My soul will be satisfied as with the richest of foods;
With singing lips my mouth will praise You."
Psalm 63:4-5

What do Blaise Pascal, (a mathematician and theologian from the 1600s) Mike Burns, (former senior pastor of Journey Community Church in San Diego) and the Rolling Stones (legendary rock band) have in common?

Each has contributed to my education on satisfaction.

We each yearn to be satisfied in life. Excitement is a plus, security is a need, but satisfaction is a deep desire all of us share. And trying to get our satisfaction from the wrong sources is the birth of most of our troubles.

Blaise Pascal wrote "There is a God-shaped vacuum in the heart of every person, and it can never be filled by any created thing. It can only be filled by God, made known through Jesus Christ."

Only God can fill up that hole. Not my husband or son, not my writing or chocolate. Only intimacy with the Father of all. All of us seek satisfaction in other things. We decorate and shop, we purchase and acquire and we raise our eyebrows when a new gadget appears on the TV.

Enter Mike Burns, my pastor a while back. In a sermon he said, "Enjoy life and what it has to offer. But only get your satisfaction from God."

I love that! Christ came that we would have abundant life complete with joy in conversations and traveling and art and food. Nothing wrong with shopping, decorating or looking into new gadgets. They are to be enjoyed with gratitude.

But they will not bring ultimate satisfaction. Nope. Only Jesus.

And of course the Rolling Stones "I Can't Get No Satisfaction" puts an exclamation point on this. Of course you can't get satisfaction, Mick! You're not looking up!

Psalm 63:5 has the answer. Only in worshipping Him will we have that soul satisfaction that causes a deep breath out and a relaxation of the heart. True joy.

Today take some time, carve out a few minutes and worship. Praise the Creator of all. Then wait a minute and experience what He'll do.

Satisfy your soul. Absolutely!

16 Let It Go

"Bear with each other and forgive whatever grievances
you may have against one another.
Forgive as the Lord forgave you."
Colossians 3:13

Do you get shed on? My dog Scooby is a shedder. He leaves his brown and gray hairs all over anyone who sits with him.

But I'm talking about people, not just animals.

Do you find yourself covered in other people's "stuff"? I know I do. And truth be told, I leave my share of excess hair on others.

My friend Lucille Zimmerman is a counselor and she says, "Brush it off like cat hair. Stop letting people stick it on you."

This past week several people felt the need to shed on me. Some of it was annoying. Some of it was hurtful.

The woman at the grocery store kept talking to the cashier when I was behind her. I was in a hurry. She looked at me and I knew she could tell. She kept talking. Leisurely.

Little hairs flew through the air and landed smack dab on my shoulders.

A new neighborhood boy showed up at our door and wanted to play with Noah. I told him we were eating dinner.

He kept talking and I said, "Go home and come back." I used a stern voice.

He said, "I don't have to obey people who are mean to me."

I smacked him and he left.

Okay, of course, I didn't hit him. But I made it clear he needed to leave immediately. He left. But as he walked away, he shed on me. In fact he covered me.

A couple of women I know have made remarks that I took a little too personally. Afterwards, I rehearsed their comments and built them up into words that crushed me. Hair everywhere.

So what's the solution?

God gives us a lent brush by way of Colossians 3:13. Bear and forgive. Or my personal interpretation – Let it Go!

Colossians 3:13 tells me to bear with the woman at the store. Maybe she was really lonely. Maybe she is just a thoughtless and selfish shopper. Not my business. But my reaction to her *is* my business. Robbie, just let it go!

The little boy that we are getting to know isn't a juvenile delinquent out to make my life miserable. It appears to me that he just doesn't have many adults in his life who say what they mean. So I need to. But taking his words personally is on me. Doesn't do any good and may end up spoiling future meals. Just let it go!

Those women, like me, often speak first and think about what they said later. Their comments stung a little, but it was I who took them in, gave them validity and grew them into stabbing wounds. Me. Time to let 'em go!

And remember the end of Colossians 3:13, "Forgive as the Lord forgave you."

I cannot imagine how much sin I've shed on God. But His reaction?

The cross.

The ultimate in letting it go.

17 We Need Elbows

"Just as each of us has one body with many members, and these members
do not all have the same function, so in Christ we who are many form
one body, and each member belongs to all the others."
Romans 12:4-5

Sometimes the "edit button" between my brain and mouth doesn't work. I have many stories of saying the wrong thing at the wrong time. With maturity, I've gotten better at using self control but I still hear inappropriate words fly out of my mouth willy-nilly.

Once when I was teaching, I stood before an auditorium of students to make an announcement. A fellow teacher had just gotten married, so I congratulated her. I heard myself saying, "Yay for marital sex!"

I saw some shocked faces but mostly just heard the laughter. Then I spied my principal's face. He was not happy.

Last night I attended my writers' meeting at Barnes and Noble. I'd never met the speaker and I was quite interested in her topic. In the middle of her speech I was in deep thought about what she was saying and apparently my face showed some confusion. She looked at me, mid-presentation, and said, "You look like you have a question. Your face is wrinkled."

The "edit button" was broken. I said, "It's gas."

My mother used to tell me "Robbie, think before you speak." She said that a lot.

Last night I heard laughter and I also heard my mother rolling over in her grave.

My personality and my personality defects are all one big, happy package that God wants to prune and use. He loves my humor, I'm sure of it and He probably giggled last night. But sometimes I have a problem reconciling my personality and my desire to be a Godly woman. See, when I picture a Godly gal I envision an impeccably dressed, wise, confident and tactful lady. I don't see a large woman who interrupts a guest speaker's presentation with wise cracks about flatulence.

You know what? I AM WRONG. God loves me just like I am. He made me. As I grow in the Lord, I want self control to be a more evident fruit of the Spirit in my life. But I also want to glorify God through the way I am. If you have committed your life to Christ, you are part of His body. And in the body of Christ, I am like the elbow, needed to support and move the arm. I will never be a hand, like Mother Theresa who touched so many. I was not made to be an eye, like Billy Graham who saw straight into peoples' hearts and identified what they needed. I am an elbow, where the funny bone is located, and I thank God for it. I pray that as you read this you will be encouraged to identify yourself as a precious part of the body of Christ, needed and loved.

Just like you are, "edit button" or not.

18 Anyone Have An Abacus?

"(Love) is not easily angered, keeps no record of wrongs."
1 Corinthians 13:6

Noah played in the same soccer league with the same coach for three years. As a result, we played the same teams occasionally. A man and his wife coached one of those teams. They annoyed me. Probably because they always won. But it also had to do with the fact that they made a point to broadcast the score out loud as if none of us in the crowd had any math skills. They did this often. Too often.

When this happened I was tempted to run up to them with an abacus and yell, "I have learned the secret of keeping score too!"

I try to feed Sarcastic Robbie less and less, hoping she will one day leave. But alas, she is still alive and well.

Announcing the score is not just relegated to annoying coaches whose team regularly defeated my son's team. In relationships, we all tend to be the play-by-play announcers from time to time. Using phrases like "Remember when you…" or "You always…" or "You never…" signal a score announcement between friends or family or spouses.

This verse in 1 Corinthians 13 puts it simply. If we want to love like God has designed us to love, we have to put down the score cards and destroy the stat records. Every day needs to be a clean slate. We love unconditionally because we make it a point to have short term memories. And we thank God for His short term memory of our sins.

If I make it a habit to keep a running list of every time someone has wronged me, it often leads to an entitlement attitude. "I don't deserve that..." "I am the center of our relationship, not you." This self absorption plants the seeds of entitlement and entitlement grows gardens of grudges.

Of course, boundaries are good. Forgiving others for hurtful actions is imperative to growing into a Godly courageous human being. But allowing others to chronically abuse us with words and actions is detrimental. How do we keep the balance? We spend time with the Father, Son and Spirit who, by their continued presence in our lives, develop in us discernment.

Loving like Jesus loved is easier said than done, as is all of the Christian life. But by seeking God and His love first, I find the act of scorekeeping or hanging onto a grudge a choice I make less and less.

Except of course, when it comes to man and wife soccer coaches who annoy me. Thank God He is not done with me yet.

19 Saying No To Bunny Sandwiches!

"...let us throw off everything that hinders and the sin that so easily entangles..." Hebrews 12:1b

On walks with Scooby, I always hold the leash tight. If my puggle happens to see a bunny, he's off. No thought. Just reaction. I am surprised he doesn't have doggie whiplash because many is the time I've had to rein in him from a bunny sandwich.

A few weeks ago, Scooby saw a bunny and took off so quickly and forcibly the leash slipped out of my grip. Within seconds, he was out of eye shot. I walked around an apartment building into a parking lot calling his name. Nothing. Then I heard a little whimper. I looked in the direction of the sound, down a long line of the backs of cars. Between a pair of them, I saw Scooby's nose. As I neared him, I found him whimpering, no bunny in sight. In fact, his leash was tangled up around the tire of a car.

When I read Hebrews 12:1, I think of Scooby all tangled up after hounding that bunny. The lure of the chase called to him and off he went, only to find himself wedged and whimpering.

Sin does that to us, doesn't it? We chase after our desires without any thought to the consequences, only to end up wedged in and immobile.

Faith requires action. But chasing the adventure of where our faith may lead is much more difficult than following our carnal whims.

Every morning I have to make a decision. The easy route that lures me like a bunny sandwich is the choice to stay on the couch, eat a donut and slip into mindless TV. The other path requires me to put on my walking shoes and take off. My faith in God assures me that putting in the time to get my body healthy will result in His blessings and the freedom to experience more of life. But to get there, I have to throw off the temptation, the laziness that would love to hinder my progress. Otherwise, I will end up entangled in exhaustion and more bad news at the doctor's office.

When I found Scooby tangled up, I laughed at my dog and then crawled under a car to unwrap the leash from the tire. He can't help chasing those bunnies, but I have the power to say no to mine.

20 Let Him Paint

"Find rest, O my soul, in God alone; my hope comes from Him."
Psalm 62:5

Once upon a time I picked up a rock and made a pledge to my King, the Master of Creativity, the Ultimate Artist.

I said, "Father, I will be a people pleaser no more. I only want to please You."

That was five years ago. The rock sits on my night stand and when I see it I am reminded that my tendency to want to please everyone is a constant temptation. Every day I must renew my desire to live for God alone.

Today I have struggled with this and today I ran across something I wrote the day I picked up that rock. I hope the Lord uses these words to encourage you to look to Him and Him alone for validation, worth and guidance.

Portrait of People Pleasing Me

HE is a great painter.

He sees my portrait, even as the canvas is blank.

He begins.

I say, "Use red."

He says, "No, not red."

"But," I say, "I like red."

"Okay." He paints with the red.

I choose green as the next color.

He says, "No green right now."

"But my teachers say green. So do my parents."

"Okay," and he paints with the green.

He chooses blue next.

"No painter, no blue next. My church says it's time for orange."

He shrugs and uses the orange.

After a bit, I say, "My boss says brown."

Without a word, the painter takes the brown and paints.

I decide to sneak a peek.

"Wow, that's me!" I say.

"Yes." He says.

"It's beautiful," I say. "You're good, but something's missing. Don't you think?"

The painter looks at me and smiles.

"Uh-huh." He says.

"What is it?" I say.

But I cut him off from answering. I go and ask my friends, my husband, my pastor. They'll know.

I bring back three pints of white, pink and purple.

He takes the paints and sets them down. Then he hugs me. He tells me he loves painting my picture. He tells me I am beautiful.

I blush and say, "Okay, but it's still missing something, so use these colors."

He takes the white, pink and purple and he paints.

I look at it again.

"It's nice. It's me. But something's missing. I don't know what. Do you?"

He doesn't say anything. I think He is waiting to see if I will answer my own question.

Finally he says, "I know what's missing."

"You do?"

"Uh-huh."

"What?"

He smiles gently, warmly and he says, "Me."

"What?" I say. "But you're doing the painting. You're in control."

"Am I?" He says.

It occurs to me that it is time to let him pick the colors.

It is time to please his vision.

Not mine.

Not anyone else's.

I say, "Paint, painter, do your thing."

A twinkle comes to his eye and he gets busy.

It's fun to watch.

After a while, he calls me over and shows me the portrait.

"Wow!" I say.

The portrait is beautiful. Nothing is missing.

"That's how you see me?" I ask him.

"That's how you are. And are becoming. And will be."

"Wow."

21 Page 430

"That He would grant you, according to the riches of His glory,
to be strengthened with might through His Spirit in the inner man."
Ephesians 3:16 (NKJ)

As I sat on our couch, I felt a book thrust into my face.

"Look. Page 430! I can't do it!"

My son Noah was now standing in front of me, eyes teary, face full of defeat.

Since our son was little bitty, we knew he possessed a love of numbers. That affection grew into a passion for math. He has always gotten great grades in this subject and we've proudly listened as teachers have bragged on his prowess.

And then…Algebra.

This year Noah is in the 6th grade but he was placed into a 9th grade level math class. And it has been difficult. I love that finally he's being really challenged, but it is difficult to watch him struggle. A month ago, at a parent/teacher conference, Mrs. Flaish told us that although Noah has a C+ she may recommend that he repeat the course next year in order to fully grasp all the concepts. This announcement destroyed Noah. But we explained that a) repeating a higher level course is not the end of the world and b) he could change this by digging in and really studying this trimester.

He's trying. But moments of discouragement creep up and land on him hard like his algebra book landed in my lap.

John, the math guy in our home, was gone. I looked at page 430 and I felt as if I were looking at hieroglyphics. I asked him a couple of questions and discovered that Noah did indeed, know *how* to do the problems, but he was frustrated with the time it took to complete them.

I prayed for him and told him he needed to discover the incredible strength God had placed in him. If he asked God and looked inside himself, he would find that his "inner man" was strong and able to finish his work. He slugged back to his room, still discouraged. I began praying that God would do His thing in my boy.

A long while later, Noah emerged from his room, now exhausted. He stood in front of me. "I finished."

I recognized this as an important moment. I flew off the couch and hugged my son and whooped it up. I told him to remember this. I patted on his chest and said, "You have so much strength in there, Noah!"

Apparently, I patted too hard and while laughing and coughing he said, "I also have asthma in there, Mom."

What grows each of us in character is our ability, our choice, to get up after we fall, isn't it? Noah has received plenty of A's in his short math career. But none of them meant as much to me as witnessing his finishing something he was convinced he could not do.

What is your Page 430? Is it finishing that project you told yourself you'd complete? Is it forgiving your friend/spouse one more time? Is it loving that sick child?

Right now, my Page 430 is making the choice to eat right and exercise. Countless times I look up at God and I thrust my heart into His face and say, "I CAN'T DO THIS!" But God never leaves us hanging and provides the strength we need to get up and keep going. Even this morning as I looked at my tennis shoes, I told God I just couldn't get up and walk. I couldn't.

But His Spirit strengthened my inner Robbie and I got up, laced the shoes and leashed the dog and off I went. It won't be the last time I ask Him for help just as there are many more challenges in my son's math career. Page 430s exist to remind us to look up and pray.

And discover the strength He's given each of us in our inner man.

22 May I Have Some More - Ish?

"Ask and it will be given to you; seek and you will find; knock and the door will be opened to you." Matthew 7:7

A couple of weeks ago, Noah taught me a new Junior High term.

He walked in from school. "Hey, Mom."

"Hi, Noah. Did you have a good day?"

"Ish."

After further investigation I discovered that "ish" is an often used expression among Noah's peers. It means "sorta" or "kinda."

Yesterday it occurred to me that we live in an "ish" world. Apathy runs rampant while passion is the exception, not the rule. I believe this is especially true in living for Jesus.

Am I passionate about God? Ish.

Do I strive each day to live for Him? Ish.

See what I mean? Ish?

When my sister Karen prays for me over the phone, she will often use another phrase, not "ish." She says, "More, Lord." I've heard this often from her but I've never really thought about it.

Today I had an epiphany. I began reading "Surprised by the Power of the Spirit" by Jack Deere and on page 15 he writes the following:

No, neither I nor my circle of friends were looking for 'something more' from God. If I had any problems at all, it was just figuring out how to give more of myself to God.

Light bulb! I have been trying to give more and more of myself to God, more passion, more service, more striving. And I've been confused when after all my efforts, I feel "ish." With the "ish" comes exhaustion or burn-out or insecurity. Today I realized it's because I've put it all on ME.

To live for Jesus with passion means to give Him more and more of myself, right? WRONG.

To live for Jesus with passion means to ask and receive more and more of Him! More, Lord!

It's a significant paradigm shift and one that relieves me of the burden of being all "Christianee."

The Father wants me to give Him my heart and my life. But to live for Him is to use His strength through the Spirit, not mine through my own efforts and flesh.

Am I passionate about God? More Lord!

Do I strive each day to live for Him? More Lord!

Ask Him for more. And don't ask like the orphan Oliver asked for more porridge: "Please sir, may I have some more?" If you ask that way, it sounds as if you are asking "May I have some more-ish?"

Ask boldly and you will receive MORE OF HIM!

23 We All Need His Flashlight

"But when he, the Spirit of truth, comes, he will guide you into all the truth..." John 16:13

"Guide me in your truth and teach me, for you are God my Savior, and my hope is in you all day long." Psalm 25:5

"The Lord will guide you always..." Isaiah 58:11

I'm in a battle in my writing right now. It's a good thing, challenging me and causing me to think through priorities and motivations. My number one need is discernment.

According to the Merriam Webster dictionary, discernment means to comprehend the obscure, or that which is hidden in darkness. Discernment isn't easy. I asked God to guide me, but when I didn't get the answer quickly, I asked other writers. Their opinions, all given with great intentions, were varied. Concerning my writing and my novel, I've heard:

Write for the Christian Market.
Write for the Secular Market.
Cut out the first 40 pages of your novel.
Write in third person instead of first.
Write in first person present, I love it!
Make your lead character more sympathetic.
I love your lead character, she is so real.
Self publish.

Wait for one of the main publishing houses.

You could be the next Christian Fanny Flagg.

Don't quit your day job, Robbie. (Well, no one actually said this one.)

Now what I'm supposed to do with my writing seems more obscure than ever.

The answer, as always, is to get back to the basics with Christ.

1) Pray – "God, guide me," is an excellent prayer.

2) Listen – We live in a noisy world. Get some place quiet, not quiet like the TV is still on in the background, but really quiet and just listen.

3) Believe that He will speak to you. If you don't know if what you are sensing is God or not, test it against the Scriptures.

4) Wait. Don't be in a hurry.

5) Walk into His blessings! When He shines His flashlight of discernment and you see the cobblestone path in front of you, don't over think it. Just go.

What if we choose the "wrong" path? One of the really cool things about God is His grace and mercy which covers us. The choice I make may look wrong because it doesn't live up to my expectations or someone else's. We are told to walk by faith, not sight. It won't always "look" right. But God is sovereign and His grace covers us no matter what road we walk down.

Are you going through a time when you need to make a choice and you just aren't sure what to do? Getting advice from others is wise, but using discernment by listening to our Lord will bring you to the right choice for YOU. He loves you and me so much. No matter what I write, God is with me, drawing me to Him.

The journey is full of joy.

24 See You At The Finish Line

"Let us run with perseverance the race marked out for us."
Hebrews 12:1c

Last week I did something I never thought I'd do. I walked in a 5K race. That's 3 miles to those of us who have no need to ever know what a 5K is. After walking each day for weeks, it occurred to me to start measuring how long I walked. Soon I discovered that I had gone over 2 miles. Then 2.5. Now I have reached 3 miles several times. Yes, I am now a bona fide athlete. Not.

I am not a fan of exercise in any way shape or form. Sometimes if I'm bored of walking, I put on a Jillian Michaels workout video instead. Jillian Michaels is the she-devil physical trainer on *The Biggest Loser.* I know that this woman is on a DVD and therefore not actually in my home. But when she instructs me to move my muscles in ways that I'm sure are illegal, she becomes very real. At least in my bitter resentment. But I don't throw the video away. I keep it, hoping that one day, I'll show Jillian, and I will be able to finish her 25 minute power sculpt. So far, after 10 to 15 minutes I hit the off button and limp around the house looking for Ben Gay. But I keep trying. I don't quit completely. At least not yet.

I mentioned that I might sign up for a 5K to my sister-in-law Lory said she said she would do it with me. Thrilled, I went to The Running Store, an establishment that I have now gone to three times. Before I started walking I looked at this building as a place for "those" people – the skinny ones who did marathons and bought stock in spandex. Now that I've frequented this establishment, I understand that "those" people are just normal folks, trying to be healthy. I'm still not one of "them" but I don't resent them. At least not as much.

with my registration for the 5K, I got a t-shirt. I registered for Lory and filled in her form. On mine, I checked the largest size available – XXL

– while Lory asked for a medium. *Um…okay…I can do this, right?* A fleeting vision ran through my mind of Lory sitting in a Lazy Boy chair waiting for me at the finish line, while I walked up with my oxygen on wheels beside me. But I dismissed the thought and turned in the forms.

After registering I looked at the day's events. 7:30 – 8:00 register. 8:15 aerobic warm-up. What? They actually think I am going to waste what precious energy I have warming up? I don't think so. While "they" do that I will look for a Lazy Boy.

8:30 race begins. When I saw the word "race" I was immediately transported to Junior High track with me finishing in last place. As I stared at the 5K form, I told myself that this 5K is not a competition for me. Adult Robbie vanquished Junior High Robbie and reasoned that my goal is to finish. Alive. With no ambulance needed. I'm not going to worry about the other Junior High girls. Well, the other participants.

Not long ago, I saw a video of a runner who was expected to win the 440 in the Olympics but tore a hamstring at the 220 yard mark. He fell down in agony. The guys with stretchers approached and he waved them off, got up and started limping to the finish line. His dad ran up beside him and helped him to the end. One of those moments that made everyone in the crowd, from all nationalities, stand to their feet and cheer on this guy's commitment and perseverance. Very moving.

If I pull a hamstring at mile marker 2, I will not get up and limp to the finish. I will whine and ask for ice cream. But I admire this young man's perseverance and I admire his dad for coming to his rescue to help him finish his race.

We all have our own races in life to run, don't we? It may be walking a child through a rebellious stage or working through a difficult season of marriage. Or it might be getting up every morning and exercising to get healthy. Whatever it is, let us all persevere.

And when we fall, our Heavenly Dad will come running up beside us, put his arm around us and help us finish. Or buy us ice cream.

25 Turn North

"You have circled this mountain long enough. Now turn north."
Deuteronomy 2:3

The Israelites were in the wilderness wandering. In Deuteronomy 2:3, God told Moses to go a different way. The circling of the mountain had to end.

I am a wanderer, and I've been circling the mountain of sugar for most of my life. God has told me clearly that it is time to go a different way. In my now twenty-five years of weight gain and weight loss, I have never completely given up desserts and cokes. I've danced around the idea, telling myself well, I'll not eat any candy until the weekend or I won't have cake again until my birthday. But it's never lasted because when I eat desserts, be it candy or cakes or cookies, then I crave candy and cakes and cookies.

Seventeen days ago, I said goodbye to sugar. And the past two weeks have been torture for me. I feel like I'm in detox and I keep looking around for Dr. Drew to come to my rescue. I've discovered just a little bit of what a hold I've allowed sugar to have on me. Not just physically either. Yesterday I wanted to reward Noah for something and my first thought was to get him some sugar. In the afternoons when I feel my energy at a lull, my first thought? Find some sugar. I stayed up watching a movie the other night and I felt restless and unfulfilled. Why? Cause I watched it with no sugar in my hand.

I hope that I keep surrendering this to God, because I also feel a freedom like I haven't ever felt. But I can only testify to the power of God in my life right now, because as I write this, I have no sugar anywhere.

Sugar is not bad. God made sugar with a grin. It's delightful. Proverbs 25:16 says "If you find honey, eat just enough - too much of it, and you will vomit." I have eaten past my share and so it's time in my life to lay off of the good stuff so I can clearly see and experience the better stuff – God's purpose for my life.

So what about you? You may not be a sugar fiend like me, but you may be circling a mountain that leads nowhere, also. Maybe it's gossip or arguing with your husband or kids. Maybe it's a drug or a holier-than-thou attitude. Ask God and He'll show you the mountain if you have one.

If you do, join me. Turn north. It's a difficult journey, let me tell you.

But oh baby, the Promised Land awaits!

26 Declare Your Independence From Fear!

"Fear not for I am with you. Be not dismayed, for I am your God. I will strengthen you, yes, I will help you. I will hold you in My righteous right hand!" Isaiah 41:10

"NO, JOHN, you are NOT going to ride a motorcycle. Ever!"

I remember saying this to John in our second year of marriage. Motorcycles scared me. To me, they were synonymous with death. John respected my wishes, but after we moved to Denver five years ago, he announced to me that he wanted to ride motorcycles.

When Noah was six, it occurred to me that fear was a huge problem for me. My fear had leaked onto him and he showed signs of fearfulness in simple childhood activities like sports. I began a long road to stomp out the fear in my life.

When John decided to ride motorcycles after we moved to Denver, the Lord had prepared me and I said "Go ahead, honey. Have fun!" Inside I was screaming. But as I walked through my fears, courage grew.

Three years ago, that courage was given its biggest test. John left to go on a motorcycle ride one morning and came back home a month later, after a serious motorcycle accident left him to battle a traumatic brain injury. God healed John completely. Before he was out of the hospital he told me, "I still want to ride."

Last week my husband rode off on his new motorcycle and I prayed, "God give me courage beyond understanding. Peace and courage." He did. A neighbor saw John ride off and asked me how I could let my husband get another bike after the accident.

1)I don't "let" my husband do anything. He's his own man and although we discuss decisions and he respects my opinion, this was his call and I support him.

2) I am tired, so tired, of living in the "what ifs" of life. Those moments steal the joy of the RIGHT NOW.

I put a picture of John and his bike on Facebook (Wanna be my Facebook friend? Look me up and I'd love it!) and I told him about another step in my growth toward courage.

He looked at me with a twinkle and asked, "How about I drive you to Five Guys Burgers for a date on the Fourth?"

"Uh….no. I'm not there yet. Watching you enjoy a motorcycle is one thing, but why in the world would I EVER want to get on one of those DEATHTRAPS??!!" Even as I said the words, it occurred to me that my journey to living in courage is far from over.

So today I hopped on the back of my husband's motorcycle and let him take me to lunch. At first I was breathing heavy, like I was going to hyperventilate. I began praying and saying Isaiah 41:10 aloud. I asked lots of questions like, "Was that a wiggle? What's that noise? How fast are you going? Do I weigh too much?"

Saint John assured me everything was fine. And then, the miracle of God's love and power in me occurred. I let go of my fear. I leaned back and joy started filling me up. When I got on the bike it was to conquer the fear. But God went beyond and gave me JOY. This surprised me. HE surprised me with the capacity to get a kick out of a motorcycle.

After our lunch, I asked John to take the long way home. During our ride, I lifted my hands to the sky and praised our God!

Want Joy? Declare your independence from fear!!

John is now planning a road trip for us...sounds fun, but we have to make sure the wills are in order. I'm still a work in progress.

Three

Joy in the Battle

27 Can I Borrow A Cup Of Sugar?

"Carry each other's burdens..."
Galatians 6:2

"Can I borrow a cup of sugar?"

It's an old adage, but one that evokes friendship, neighborliness and even security. I enjoy the thought that if indeed, I am in the middle of baking my famous chocolate chip cookies and find that my pantry is running low on an ingredient, I can run next door and ask for supplies. And I have.

Isn't it interesting that having back up, even in the trivial activity of baking, brings security? Great neighbors provide security. Lousy ones steal it away.

The last couple of weeks my level of personal security has been challenged. Will my husband be okay after his accident? Will our lives change? If so, how? But I've found that my brothers and sisters in Christ have brought me security. Like great neighbors.

In fact, a few times I have gone to my neighbors in Jesus and asked a deep spiritual question.

"Can I borrow some of your faith?"

And like great neighbors, they've helped. They've seen those moments in me where I've been filled with panic and doubt. They've gone to their Biblical cupboards and loaned me a cup of truth.

"Robbie," they've said, "God is in control. He loves John even more than you do. He'll get better. He will."

I've received their faith and added it to my heart. The result has been a recipe for perseverance. Perseverance to walk through the journey of John's motorcycle accident.

We need each other, don't we? If you are experiencing a lack of faith, don't succumb to guilt. It's useless. Look around.

Ask a neighbor for a cup of faith.

28 Never Alone

"…knowing that your brothers around the world
are undergoing the same kinds of suffering…"
1 Peter 5:9

Her name is Bianca. She is lovely and fun, overweight and blond. Laughter comes easy for her, but so do tears. And right now, Bianca is going through a time of suffering.

The verse above, 1 Peter 5:9, has given me such comfort the past three weeks as I have dealt with my husband's motorcycle accident and extended stay in ICU and rehab. It reminds me that I am not alone. I am not the only one that has ever dealt with a husband in the hospital. I am not the only woman married to a man with a wild heart who loves motorcycles. Realizing this consoles me and keeps me from going to the "poor me I am the only one" scenario.

So here's what I do. I imagine a woman, like me, who is going through the exact same thing I am going through right now. She lives in Europe somewhere and her husband is a wonderful man with a warped sense of humor. Her son is almost 10. Sound familiar?

I think about her and I pray for her. I know I have created her in my mind, but at the same time I KNOW she is real. Maybe she isn't exactly like me, but God assures me that somewhere a woman lives and is suffering with the same set of circumstances as I am. As I pray for Bianca in that London or Paris hospital, sitting in frustration and wondering if this will ever end, somehow I am stronger.

It works that way doesn't it? When we are weak and we turn our thoughts toward someone else or serve someone else, the Lord's strength infuses us and gives us perspective.

Bianca's husband will recover. And Bianca is going to be fine. This season of suffering will end for her and like a pruned rose she will blossom with new bursts of color and beauty and joy.

I am connected to Bianca and so many other women right now who are looking to God for strength. We form a garden of multi-colored roses, lifting our bouquets of gratitude to the Lord Jehovah who wastes nothing. Even suffering.

Join us. Hang in there and remember your brothers and sisters throughout the world. You are not alone.

29 Who Do You Trust?

"Stop trusting in man, who has but a breath in his nostrils.
Of what account is he?" Isaiah 2:22

(Jesus speaking)
"Do not let your hearts be troubled. Trust in God; trust also in me."
John 14:1

Five months ago my husband John suffered a traumatic brain injury due to a motorcycle crash. He also dealt with a blood clot in his lungs and an infected leg which led to surgery.

Today John is fine. In God's great mercy, He healed my husband. Completely. Go God! As we walked through the months of recovery God showed Himself faithful. But trusting God in the day to day battles proved difficult.

My brother Perry's words guided me from the onset. After John's accident he told me, "Listen Rob. Listen carefully. The doctors and nurses are going to give you all sorts of predictions and prognosis. That's their job. But don't bank on their words. Don't believe them. Trust God. No one else."

The other day I looked at my notes from the past months and began to giggle at actual quotes I jotted down from doctors and nurses.

- "I think he will bounce back quickly. Probably 3 or 4 days and he'll be out of here. He might need a day or two of rehab." (1st night – Trauma surgeon)
- "He's so agitated. He will probably wake up violent and cussing you out so get ready." (Nurse – Day 2)

- "You need to be prepared for a long, long road." (Nurse – Day 4)
- "This may take a while."(Trauma surgeon – Day 5)
- "Wow, he seems to be improving quickly." (Doctor – Day 6)
- "He can go to rehab tomorrow." (Trauma surgeon – Day 7)
- "No one goes straight to rehab from ICU – so be prepared – he may have a major backslide." (Nurse)
- "He's doing well." (Doctor at rehab)
- "He's not doing as well as he should." (Doctor at rehab)
- "We checked for blood clots and he doesn't have any." (Saturday)
- "He has a blood clot in his lungs." (The next day – Sunday)
- "He should be in rehab for seven days tops."
- "We're thinking at least one more week – probably next Tuesday."
- (Monday night) "He's not ready to go home, maybe Thursday."
- "Your blood thinner level needs to be between 2 and 3 – right now it's 1.8. Robbie, watch him very closely!"
- "Today your blood level is 7.3. This is VERY DANGEROUS AND SCARY."
- "It looks like he'll be in cognitive therapy for 6 to 10 weeks. Maybe he'll be able to go back to work after that."
- (5 days later) "He can go back to work next week!"
- "The leg wound looks terrific, right on track!"
- "We need to operate. The wound is infected."

I am very thankful to the medical community. Without medicine, doctors and nurses I would've lost my best friend in the world. Thank God for them. But while their words are important I've learned again to choose to trust God.

Join me. Trust God and God Alone.

30 Lightning Beats Flames Every Time

"Therefore, take up the full armor of God,
so that you will be able to resist in the evil day,
and having done everything, to stand firm...
in addition to all, taking up the shield of faith
with which you will be able to extinguish
all the flaming arrows of the evil one."
Ephesians 6:13 and 16

Flaming Arrows Happen. This would be a good bumper sticker.

We don't have control over the enemy's artillery attacks or his aim. Satan's job is to attack constantly and consistently. He is subtle. C. S. Lewis' book, *The Screwtape Letters*, is a series of letters in which a mentor demon gives his nephew Wormwood detailed advice on various methods to promote sin and undermine faith in a Christian.

The enemy wants to get us when we are sleeping, eating, writing, watching TV, talking to friends, driving in the car. He loves to get us when we are sitting and thinking.

He is a master archer with his bulls-eye on our souls. The arrows carry discouragement, disillusion, hopelessness, pride, arrogance, self loathing, selfishness, apathy and fear. He owns them all.

We can't control his evil intent, his perfectly precise bow or his massive quiver full of arrows.

However, we can control how we defend ourselves. We can stand firm and carry a shield of faith. Believing that God is in control and He will be faithful to carry us through every situation.

In Ephesians 6:16, Paul is talking about the Roman soldiers who carried large oblong shields, made of wood but covered in leather which was soaked in water to quench the flaming arrows the enemy shot at them.

When we put on our armor each day, picking up the shield of faith is vital. We are declaring that faith in God and His power is our protection.

Paul wrote in 2 Thessalonians 3:3 "But the Lord is faithful and He will strengthen and protect you from the evil one."

In fact, God wants to rescue us. I love Psalm 18, in which David paints a picture of God "soaring on the wings of the wind" to come and rescue us.

Psalm 18:14 says "He shot His arrows and scattered the enemies. Great bolts of lightning and routed them."

Hmm…So the enemy has his flaming arrows. But God's weapons are much bigger than Satan's arrows of fire. My God uses bolts of lightning. So there you go.

God's lightning bolts beat the liar's flaming arrows every time. Comparing the two makes it easier to put on our shields of faith. We are on the winning side.

31 Hang On!

"The righteous cry out, and the Lord hears,
And delivers them out of all their troubles,
The Lord is near to those who have a broken heart,
and saves such as have a contrite spirit."
Psalm 34:15-16

"Sometimes **all** that God requires of you is to **hang on to Him.**"

Normally I'm pretty self-focused. I'm trying to allow God to change this in me. But every once in a while I will have a day or a week in which I feel overwhelmed by the problems other folks are having.

This past week that's how I've felt. Maybe it's because I am trying to practice the presence of God. Maybe when you or I make the choice to consciously allow God to be part of our daily lives, compassion naturally infuses us.

So as I have spoken to several people this past week, I have found myself feeling awful for them.

I've thought about my toughest times. Watching my mother die, spending the first two weeks of Noah's life in the NICU, working through the process of rebuilding our marriage seven years ago, and choosing faith as John recovered from his motorcycle crash a year ago January.

And I've tried to remember what people did for me that honestly helped me. Number one was prayer. Number two was their presence. Not the words, but the fact that they took time to just be with me while I was in pain. And number three was service. What a blessing to have someone clean your house or bring you a meal. All three helped me so much.

But someone said something to me that really helped me get through. His words gave me the grace to not worry about being perfect or "Christianee" during a rough time. He said to me, "Robbie, sometimes all that God requires of you is to hang on to Him."

I want to pass that on to those of you who are hurting. Hang on to God. Just hang on.

You who are dealing with addiction, hang on to His love.

You who are facing bankruptcy and foreclosure. Hang on.

You who are facing surgery. Hang on.

You who are grieving the loss of someone very special. Hang on to His presence.

You who are angry with your spouse and don't see how you'll stay. Hang on to Him.

You who are watching your child fight a horrible illness. Just hang on.

Hang on with white knuckles and shallow breath. Hang on even if your emotions are telling you to run away from God. Hang on.

After that man told me to hang on he added, "And someday Robbie, when you aren't hanging on to God for dear life, well, then it's your turn to encourage others to hang on."

So if you are not in a crisis, look around and tell someone who is hurting to hang on tight.

He won't let go.

32 Valleys

"Though I walk through the valley of the shadow of death,
I will fear no evil. For Thou art with me."
Psalm 23:4

This week I spent a few days in the valley. Do you know what I mean? We've all spent time there.

The valley is a place of sorrow. Sometimes valleys are long and crowded with tall prickly grass. Grief that doesn't seem to end. Sometimes valleys are short and tender. The surrounding hills slope with despair and disappointment.

I dropped into a valley when I heard God tell me no last Thursday. I wanted something desperately. He just said, "No." For a couple of days I felt a dream had died. Then after my crying stopped, I realized it was just a redirection. But it was still a painful valley.

In Psalm 23:4 David writes, "Though I walk through the valley of the shadow of death, I will fear no evil, for thou art with me."

Psalm 23 is often used to comfort those who've lost someone. But it's not just for funerals. Those powerful words are for anyone in a valley. The shadows of death can fill the corners of our hearts through despair, disappointment and heartache, not just the actual passing of someone. In the valley, evil lurks. The enemy loves to jump on us when we are in a valley, hoping to whisper nefarious lies. Enough to fill our vulnerable hearts with doubt.

But God's presence is there, too. If we practice living in His presence while in the valleys, growth and peace multiply.

In fact, if you look at Psalm 23 you see that God is at work in the valley. He makes us lie down and rest when we're in the valley. He prepares a banquet for us, even in the midst of the enemy, and nurtures us. He fills us up for what's to come, so much our hearts overflow. He anoints us with oil.

In the valley, He restores our souls.

Still hurts. Sunday I didn't want to go to church, so I went to a coffee shop instead. Sitting with my latte, I felt God pulling me to go. I called John and told him I'd meet him.

I walked into the sanctuary and I heard these words being sung: "As I wait, You make me strong." I sat down and cried.

Have you been in a valley lately? Walk through it clinging to the King. Don't fear the enemy or believe his lies. For God art with you. Practice living in His presence.

And cry a lot.

33 Remember

"When my soul fainted within me I remembered the Lord
And my prayer came unto Thee, into thy holy temple."
Jonah 2:7 (King James Version)

After being in Sunday school class for a few weeks, in which we're studying the Minor Prophets, the prevailing lesson has been this: *I have so much to learn about the Bible.* But it's an exciting and interesting journey.

Right now we are studying Jonah, and last Sunday chapter 2, verse 7 jumped off the page at me. I asked the teacher what Jonah meant when he said "When my soul fainted" and he explained that it was that moment when Jonah was at his lowest. I'm sure being inside a huge fish helped the process. I like the next phrase, too. "I remembered the Lord." After he was swallowed by a whale of a set of circumstances he looked up and remembered who was in charge. It's too easy to forget that, isn't it?

The past few weeks I have been especially concerned about some friends. The empathy of my heart burst on Sunday. I cried and I asked God, "Why?" As I sat on my porch and prayed, all I heard was Jonah 2:7. Then I wrote the following:

My soul faints within me,
I remember God.

A friend's nephew was murdered.
What God? He was only 23.

My soul faints within me,

I remember God.

Jan is back in the hospital with an infection.
What God? Again?
Tonya's son was rushed to the hospital,
A virus attacked his heart.
The next day her husband was in a car accident.
Now he's in the ICU.
What God? What are you up to?

My soul faints within me,
I remember God.

My dear friend in San Francisco has cancer,
Doctor's appointments fill her calendar.
God, are you listening? What's happening?

My soul faints within me,
I remember God.

I am in a state of contentment,
Life is going great.
Why God? Why me?

Jonah disobeys.
He's thrown off a ship.
A fish swallows him.
He prays,
"My soul faints within me,
I remember God."

You, my God, are El Elyon,
You're in charge, You allow, You control.
I don't get it.
I don't understand.

But...
I remember You God. And maybe that's all You want.
I look up. I praise.
Even as my soul faints.

34 He Is For You

"A cheerful heart is good medicine..." **Proverbs 17:22**

My compliment of the week: "Robbie, the thing I admire about you is you're not afraid to humiliate yourself."

I laughed and laughed. In context, it was a compliment and I took it that way. But the way she put it was so funny.

When we walk through any battle, one weapon we must not lose sight of is the ability to laugh. Laughter has girded me in many difficult situations. In fact, when I am especially challenged, I look for reasons to laugh.

Last night, when my friend gave me this compliment, I agreed with her. We were talking about the gym and my attitude of just being me there. It's difficult enough for an obese woman to go into a gym, but if I add insecurity to the mix, it is excruciating. It helps that I'm 50, because I truly care less now about other people's opinions of me more than ever in my life. Freedom is the result.

When I first met my personal trainer, this was our conversation:

Me: Do you know CPR?

Mona: Yes.

Me: Have you ever done it?

Mona: Yes, and we have a portable defibrillator here.

Me: Have you used it?

Mona: Yes, last year an elderly woman's heart gave out and I worked on her until the ambulance came.

Me: Did she make it?

Mona: Yes.

Me: Where do I sign?

I think having no fear of humiliating myself comes from the choice to laugh at myself. In my life, I've had plenty of practice.

I went to a bridal shower once and didn't know it was a lingerie shower. Everyone's gifts were beautiful negligees and such. She opened up my present to find an electric knife.

I was the guest of honor at a banquet once and I sat between my date Larry and the entertainment Gary. During the meal, I got to coughing and threw up. In trying to flee, I threw up on both Larry and Gary.

Two weeks ago, I went to a parent teacher conference at Noah's Middle School. We walked around the cafeteria to different tables each teacher occupied. At one table, I sensed my chair was a bit squishy. In mid-conference, my chair collapsed and I hit the ground. I was embarrassed but decided to laugh at it. Afterwards, I kept saying in a Jerry Seinfeld voice, "It was the chair. They had a squishy chair!"

Friday is the end of the Mayan calendar and the end of the world, "they" say. I don't believe this for one second, but as a dieter I am always sniffing out justifications for eating treats. Can there be any reason more tailor-made for me than the world is ending on Friday? Sigh.

So as you can see, fodder for laughing at myself is a plenty. And laughing at life is a gift we can all give ourselves, especially in times when the enemy of our hearts wants us to live in hopeless despair.

Today, I hope you'll look for a reason to laugh. When you find it, enjoy it and relish it. The Great Physician will use it to soothe your soul as you walk through your battles. Why? Because He is for you.

35 No Black Dress For Me

"Where, O death, is your victory?
Where, O death, is your sting?" 1 Corinthians 15:55

When I was four, my playmate Prissy died in a car accident. One of my earliest memories is the moment my mom told me that Prissy went to be with Jesus.

I lost my beloved Granny when I was 12 and my Grandma Mamie when I was 21.

During my junior high and high school years, I lost seven friends, including a guy I dated.

I've lost teacher friends and students. Two of my neighbors committed suicide. Several relatives, some close and some not, have died.

And of course, my beloved parents are both deceased.

A few years ago I was teaching at a Christian high school and I shared with my students that I've had a lot of experience with death – two people died right in front of me. I've been to way too many funerals.

When I told my class this, one of my students, as only a high school girl can, looked at me in complete sincerity and asked, "Mrs. Iobst, how are you not crying all the time?"

My answer was just as sincere.

"I do cry sometimes, but I live a life of joy because I'll never attend Jesus' funeral."

On Good Friday we take a day and remember in gratitude the mystery of unconditional love and sacrifice. We imagine the pain Jesus endured and the choice He made to die in order that you and I might truly live.

And then on Easter we celebrate! We celebrate the One we never need to mourn. The One who lives eternally and who offers each of us the gift of eternal life. I will see many of those I've lost because they accepted Christ's sacrifice and chose to live for Him.

It truly is extraordinary, isn't it? We serve a RISEN SAVIOR! We'll never go to His funeral.

Happy Resurrection Day!

He is risen; He is risen indeed!

36 Living In A Might Situation

"And he will be called Wonderful Counselor, Mighty God,
Everlasting Father, Prince of Peace."
Isaiah 9:6

I might lose my house.

I might be quite sick.

My husband might lose his job.

My child might get rejected.

Might, Might, Might.

The "might" situations come often in life. Sometimes they usher us into a valley where desperation for God's help grows like the wild flowers in a meadow. And sometimes they are precursors to a trip to the mountain of gratitude, having missed bad news.

I am in a "might" situation right now. It's a precarious place, where the fear of the unknown knocks on my door often. But I don't have to let him in. I can make the choice to look at "might" in a totally different way.

Might has two basic definitions: 1) Possibly 2) Power

You and I have the freedom to choose how we deal with waiting for news, be it bad or good. We can live in the realm of possibly, which is like balancing on a moving log in water. Could go this way or could go that way but while I'm waiting I need to move my feet frantically, hoping to control the outcome.

We can also choose to live in the realm of power, which is like standing on unmoving boulder. I still don't know how it will go, but while I'm waiting I stand confidently on the ROCK, leaving the outcome to God, the Mighty God!

In practical terms, I use the Word of God to tell the enemy to go away when thoughts of possible bad news attack me and tempt me to fantasize about the worst possible situation. If I dwell, I get stuck in fear which leads to depression. The Word of God keeps me focusing on Mighty God and this moment right now!

I also don't waste time wondering about the "mights." I could probably spend most of a day just sitting and conjuring all the horrible things that "might" happen. So I remain busy, working and focusing on the tasks God has laid before me TODAY.

If you are not in a "might" situation, you will be someday. When it happens, remember that His Might is more powerful than any "might" situation. Today, this day, has so many wonderful gifts. Open them up, one at a time, and enjoy life right now. The "mights" are tools by the enemy to distract you from the Might of the One who is in control!

37 Turn The Page

"We can make our plans, but the LORD determines our steps."
Proverbs 16:9 (NLT)

Not every story ends the way we want it to, but God is still good.

- 11 years ago, I began to dream about ending my teaching career to write and speak.
- 6 years ago, I quit teaching.
- 5 years ago, we moved to Denver and I began writing and speaking professionally.
- 3 ½ years ago, I landed a literary agent.

During the past 3 ½ years (with my agent) I submitted a nonfiction memoir that made it to 2 publishing boards (a cool accomplishment in the writing biz) but it was rejected by those 2 houses as well as 8 others. I wrote another nonfiction book on fear that went nowhere because I did not have credentials or platform. This past year, I finished my first full length novel.

A week ago Monday, I wrote a Joyvotion - a love letter from God. I planned on sending it out as I usually do on Wednesday and Thursday, but God said to me quite clearly, "Send it out now, today, for that one woman who needs it."

I envisioned a woman who might be dreading Valentine's Day be they alone or lonely in a marriage. I sent it out and promptly got 3 emails saying, "Thank you, but it's not Wednesday."

Then, I received an email from my agent telling me she couldn't sell my novel and she'd decided to release me from our agent/writer relationship. Ouch. By the way, I respect her and have no hard feelings at all toward her.

But I did cry. In fact, I felt my heart break a little. My thoughts? *Am I just not good enough, God? Should I just quit this? I have no idea what to do next.*

I called my beloved. He comforted me and told me he believed in me. I mentioned I'd just sent out a Joyvotion. He said, "I know, I got it. But it's not Wednesday."

I smiled through my blubbering. "God told me to send it out this morning for that one woman who'd need it."

John replied, "That was you, Robbie."

I hung up and read the love letter again as if God wrote it just for me. And I sobbed like a little girl, as I crawled up into my Abba Daddy's lap.

This weekend, I'm going to a cabin in the pines to hang out with God for 2 days. No phone, TV, or computer. Just me and Jesus. A wonderful date or a WAAWG (Weekend Almost Alone with God.) I can't wait. Just like the love letter, He'll speak to my heart and tell me what's next.

I write this not to say poor me, but to encourage you that wherever you are in your story, God is good and He loves you. Period. Getting rejected by my agent felt horrible, like reading a sad ending full of tears and broken hearts.

But God will use it for great things. It might be a wonderful chapter ending that needed to be written just like it played out, so the next chapter can unfold exactly as God, the Author of all, wants.

If you have gotten bad news lately, take courage. He loves you with a fervent, unending love.

And your story, like mine, goes on.

Crawl into your Abba Daddy's lap and He will help you turn the page.

38 You'll Need A Tent Peg And A Hammer

"But Jael, Heber's wife, picked up a tent peg and a hammer and went quietly to him (Sisera) while he lay fast asleep, exhausted. She drove the peg through his temple into the ground, and he died."
Judges 4:21

Jael is one of my favorite women in the Bible. Read Judges 4 for the entire story, but to summarize, God used this woman to take out a really bad guy. Imagine Osama Bin Laden being killed by one female Navy seal.

I am a pacifist by nature and choice, so I don't necessarily rejoice when our enemies or convicted criminals are killed. But I understand that "putting to death" is an action that God used all through the Bible and uses today.

Consider Colossians 3:5: "Put to death, therefore, whatever belongs to your earthly nature: sexual immorality, impurity, lust, evil desires and greed, which is idolatry."

Paul doesn't instruct us to reason with our sins or hope they'll change. He says very simply – put them to death.

When I think of the sins I consistently deal with, number one is eating emotionally instead of going to God. I seek comfort, joy and numbness in eating. Food is fuel, but I've perverted it to be much more. I am on a journey to end this. It may take my entire life but I will keep fighting.

One thing that helps me in this battle is to remember Jael and her profound courage and decisiveness. Imagine her in that tent with the sleeping Sisera. She had to be stealth-like to come upon him and not wake him up. Jael possessed no wishy-washiness as she approached Sisera with the tent peg and the hammer. She made a decision and she did it. Wham! Not pretty, and definitely not passive or pacifistic.

Sin in our lives needs to be put to death. When we play around with it and fail to realize its seriousness, we fall prey to its dire consequences and pervasive wickedness.

The other day I was tempted to eat something that was not fuel and was not a blessing from God to me at that moment. It was only a way to numb myself from dealing with a situation. The Spirit brought Jael to mind. I was inspired to get my tent peg and hammer and go to town. "Get behind me Satan!" And WHAM! I put it to death. Someday I'll look up Jael in Heaven and thank her for her fearless heart. She's only mentioned in the Bible 6 times, all of which are in Judges 4 and 5, but her influence is great.

The last time she's named is Judges 5:24: "Most blessed of women be Jael, the wife of Heber the Kenite, most blessed of tent-dwelling women."

Most blessed, indeed. Today, fellow sinners, get your tent peg and hammer and get busy in the name of Jesus. With a little nod to Jael.

39 Remember Who You Are

"In the spring, at the time when kings go off to war, Joab led out the armed forces... but David remained in Jerusalem..."
1 Chronicles 20:1

" 'The Lion King.' A perfect example."

"What? How?" I'd been talking to my husband about identity.

He brought up a Disney movie. (The source of many great lessons.)

John went on to explain. In the movie, "The Lion King" Mufasa appears to Simba in a vision and says (in that deep voice of James Earl Jones) "Remember who you are!" Simba thought his father's death was his fault and therefore he wasn't worthy to be the king. So he tried to escape his life by adapting the philosophy of a warthog and meerkat – Hakuna Matata. Simba forgot who he was and needed reminding.

Are you like me and find yourself forgetting your identity?

I'm not talking about an occupation or a position in a family. I'm talking who you and I are in Christ. **Ephesians** 1 spells it out. Who am I? **I am redeemed, forgiven, blessed, accepted and chosen.** (Among other adjectives.) When we forget who we are we adapt philosophies the enemy brings. Lies that take us to that place of thinking and believing we are less than who we are.

King David, a man after God's own heart, forgot who he was. 1 Chronicles 20:1 says, "In the spring when kings went to war..." David didn't go out and battle. Instead he stayed home and had an affair with Bathsheba and had her husband killed. He forgot he was a king, and his choices led to tragedy.

So how do we remember? We remind ourselves daily. We ask the Spirit to remind us. We remind others, and by doing so, remind ourselves. You, the one reading this! Let me remind you WHO YOU ARE!

If you have asked Jesus to forgive your sins and lead your life, you are:

- **REDEEMED!** If you are redeemed, don't walk around in guilt. You are HIS. He bought you with a price on that cross.
- **FORGIVEN!** If you are forgiven, you can't go around binding yourself to tiny dreams and tasks because you are not worthy of a bigger life. You are forgiven completely. So live in freedom and go big!
- **BLESSED!** If you are blessed, don't go around living life like a victim of circumstances. Hard times and trials come, but you are not a victim! You are a victor through Christ because He has blessed you with every spiritual blessing!
- **ACCEPTED!** If you are accepted, you can't go around in insecurity feeling uniquely bad or in pride, especially gifted. You are accepted just as you are, not because of anything you do or don't do, but because of Jesus. Your acceptance is because of God and His character, not your failings or successes.
- **CHOSEN!** If you are chosen, don't go around feeling like what you have to offer is not important to your children, spouse, and coworkers. God chose YOU to live the life you have. So stand up tall and keep in touch with the One who chose you to go for it!

Fellow sojourner for the Lord, I implore you. In the midst of grief, remember who you are. In the midst of going through a job loss or divorce, remember who you are. In the midst of a promotion or a dream coming true, remember who you are!

Now think it to yourself using James Earl Jones' voice: (Cause when he speaks we listen.) "Remember who you are!"

Four
Joy in Family

40 Mad Skills

"Therefore put on the full armor of God,
so that when the day of evil comes,
you may be able to stand your ground,
and after you have done everything, to stand...
Take the helmet of salvation
and the sword of the Spirit, which is the word of God."
Ephesians 6:13 and 17

I walked into the middle of a deadly war. Using agile moves and quick light saber thrusts, Luke Skywalker was battling Darth Vader.

"Noah, John!"

The battle subsided.

"I'm going to the store. Be back in a minute."

As I walked out the door, the galactic mêlée continued.

When I came home, the skirmish had ended. Luke Skywalker was outside playing with some friends and Darth Vader was nowhere to be seen. Instead I found Jabba the Hut sitting in his easy chair.

He muttered, "Your son. Light saber. Mad skills."

Noah has played with light sabers his entire life. He started with the plastic ones that easily dent and bend. Now he owns two collectable life-size ones, complete with glowing lights and whirring sounds.

As followers of Christ, we each have our own "light saber." The sword of the Spirit is a mighty weapon and the only offensive weapon in the armor of God. And as Ephesians 6:17 explains, it is the Word of God.

Jesus modeled his sword skills when he was tempted in the wilderness by the enemy. Three times he was tempted and three times he answered with Scripture. He taught us to fight back with the Words of the Father. This is swordplay at its best.

Years ago, John and I went through a horrible time in our marriage. We considered divorce but instead we decided to try to reconcile. During that journey, God told me to quit talking to John about anything spiritual. So I bit my tongue often, and for three months I didn't talk about church, the Bible, prayer or anything related. Instead, God told me to get three 3 by 5 cards and write passages of Scripture on each. I used them to pray over John, Noah and me daily. Sometimes two or three times a day.

I learned some sword skills. And in the realm that we can't see, I did battle for my family. God honored our efforts and restored our marriage.

It is crucial to use the Bible every day, not just in times of crisis. **This takes work.** Opening the Word of God one day a week is like picking up your sword occasionally. You won't win many battles if you don't practice.

As I type these words I pray for you reading this and for me writing it. Let's take this battle seriously. Let's USE the Word of God each day when we are attacked with discouragement or fear *and* when we want to give thanks or praise.

Wouldn't it be so cool to hear God say these words about you? "Look at my child. Sword of the Spirit. Mad skills."

41 He Sees The Broken Windows

"She gave this name to the LORD who spoke to her: "You are the God who sees me," for she said, "I have now seen the One who sees me."
Genesis 16:13
El Roi – The God Who Sees

When the doorbell rang, John was surprised to see George and his mom. He knew they were neighbors, but he'd never met them.

A little while later, after George and his mom left, Noah came bouncing into our home.

"Check-in!"

"Noah, I need to ask you about something."

"What?" Noah had that I-have-to-get-back-to-playing look.

"George and his mom came over and told me about a broken window."

Noah's joy vanished and tears welled up in his eyes.

"Noah, did you break one of their windows?"

Through his sobs, Noah explained it was true. He'd accidentally broken it while throwing a golf ball to George.

Soon after, I walked in and was made privy to the news.

"I agreed that we would pay for half of the new window." John announced.

"When did this happen?" I asked.

John paused. "Apparently two months ago."

"What!? Noah, why didn't you tell us in June?" My face flushed.

"'Cause I knew I'd be in big trouble," Noah's eyes stared at the floor, his tears wetting our carpet.

This was one of those moments I am grateful to have a partner in raising this little man. I stood silent, deciding exactly how I was going to ensure my son that he'd assumed correctly. He *was* in big trouble. But John saw this as a teaching moment.

"Noah, we love you no matter what you do. You broke a window. That happens. But I am disappointed that you kept this a secret."

John explained that keeping secrets is like carrying a big bag of rocks. It's a burden. In keeping this secret, Noah only hurt his own heart and made it heavy. John talked about how no one can keep a secret from God because He doesn't want us to ever feel burdened by trying to hide the truth from Him. Noah seemed to understand. We'll know more as he gets older.

That night I started to wonder if I keep secrets from God. Do I try to hide things from Him because I know I'll get in "big trouble?" Many times in my life I have kept myself from God, even though I knew He was omniscient.

El Roi is a name of God used by Hagar in Genesis, meaning "The God who sees me." He does. He sees me sitting here typing. He saw Noah when that golf ball went sailing. He sees us in those moments when we choose selfishness. He sees us when we come to the point of crumpling up before Him in repentance.

El Roi sees. So why do we hide? The answer? We don't comprehend that **God will love us no matter what we do.** I still love Noah. No amount of broken windows will ever change that.

And El Roi still loves Noah, John and me. He loves you. **He sees you.**

42 Can You Spell Pain?

"…but we also rejoice in our sufferings,
because we know that suffering produces perseverance;
perseverance, character; and character, hope."
Romans 5:3-4

I remember clearly experiencing one of the most harrowing, anxiety-producing events of my mommy-hood. At one point I told John, "I need a defibrillator."

Noah's school-wide spelling bee.

My son sat in the midst of twenty-one spellers, all fourth and fifth graders. Each time it was Noah's turn to spell, I would grab my husband's hand and pray and breathe, not necessarily at the same time. Four tense rounds passed with nine children eliminated.

During the fifth round, Noah was given the word harness. I squeezed John's hand and felt a stroke approaching. My left side felt numb. Noah spelled the word correctly and I was instantly healed.

I've seen the televised National Spelling Bee and I've chuckled at how serious everyone takes it. But experiencing a spelling bee with my child center stage is quite different than making fun of the process from home. I'd love to ask the parents of those spellers questions like:

Have you started blood pressure medicine since this process began?

Has any parent ever attempted to choke the winner's parents?

In the sixth round, Noah was given the word devise and he began the word with d-i.

He was the twelfth person to sit down. I looked at Noah and gave him a compassionate smile. He stared at me with such hurt and then looked down, obviously disappointed. After a few more rounds, a fourth grade girl won.

After Noah sat down, I felt relieved and sad. I was angry we hadn't stayed up every night until midnight practicing. And I was curious how he would live through this devastation. Okay, I wondered how *I would live* through this devastation.

John noticed I was tearing up and whispered, "You may cry all you want after you take Noah home and go to your room alone. Until then, you *may not* cry."

So, instead of crying we did what we've done at countless soccer games. John and I looked at Noah and when his eyes met ours, we did the wave. Noah shook his head and grinned. A little.

When Noah came over after the bee, John kissed his head and told him we were proud of him. This is when Noah started crying. And then he reached out his arms and stepped toward us for a big "Family Hug!" Simultaneously we said, "Where's Scooby?" and laughed. Noah's tears stopped when he began playing with friends.

Just the other day I told a young mom that God molds our children's characters through pain. Our job is to let them experience pain, instead of always rescuing them when they feel discomfort.

I wanted to rescue my boy. I wanted him to win so I could see that joy in his eyes. But it wasn't a day for that kind of victory. It was a day for pain.

I survived the stress. The bee is a memory. But I know the work that God wants to do in Noah *and me* is ongoing. Every once in a while God sprinkles just a little pain into the mix of who He wants my son to be. Can you spell perseverance?

43 The Joy Of A Dog

"Do not grieve, for the joy of the LORD is your strength."
Nehemiah 8:10

I write this Joyvotion from the hospital. And even though I'm in a bit of a stressful situation, I feel His joy. It's my strength. Thinking how we came to be here gives me joy and strength too.

To our dog Scooby, sickness emits the same perfumed scent as bacon. At least that's been our family joke. Whenever I've been ill, Scooby nuzzles up to me and loves on me. Extra. He can tell when I'm not feeling good.

But in the past three years whenever Noah has been sick, he hasn't snuggled extra with the boy. Until Monday night.

Noah came home Friday afternoon not feeling well. He was sick all weekend but the cold didn't affect his asthma until Monday. He used his inhaler several times. That night I stayed up late, with Scooby by my side, to enjoy "Dancing with the Stars" on DVR. The males in my home refuse to watch it with me.

At about midnight, Scooby bounced up from his sleep and looked at me curiously. He tilted his head and straightened it. I had no idea what he wanted.

I casually said, "Scooby, we'll go to bed soon."

He jumped down and left. I thought he was going to his bed. We'd taken it from Noah's room and put it in ours because Noah was sick. Ten minutes later, I went to my room and noticed Scooby wasn't in his bed. I looked around and then went into Noah's room. Scooby lay cuddled up to Noah's side.

"Scooby, get down."

He wouldn't go. I tried to push and pull him but the dog wouldn't budge. He just stared at me. Scooby's never displayed this behavior before. Noah woke up and immediately went to get his inhaler. Thirty minutes later I was on the phone with the doctor and then we went to the ER.

Scooby knew.

Asthma is one of those sicknesses that require judgment calls. You don't know how bad it is sometimes. Monday night, John and I were on the fence about the seriousness of Noah's lungs. Scooby knew and brought it to our attention.

Yep, Lassie told us Timmy was in the well.

This morning, Wednesday, Noah is having a chest ex-ray done. We may go home today and we may not. I wish Scooby were here. Maybe he could tell us.

A couple of friends and I were talking the other day about whether animals would be in heaven. My vote is absolutely. John's Revelation of Heaven included horses and birds. And beyond that, I believe that God would want those of us who are blessed by animals to have that joy in the afterlife. Just like I believe Heaven will contain coconut cream pie and great moments of game playing laughter, I believe dogs will be there, too.

For now we take joy in the pleasures God has offered right here, right now. Although the last several days have been an ordeal for Noah, he's been a trooper, too. I asked him this morning if he was ready to go home today. He took a minute and thought about this.

"Mom, I like this hospital room. This bed is fun and the food they serve here is great. But I want to go home. I'll get to be with my friends at home. And Scooby." When we go home, Scooby will get extra treats. That's one of his joys.

44 Ding! It's Ready!

"Love does not behave rudely, does not seek its own..."
1 Corinthians 13:5

Love is all about the microwave oven. Let me explain.

John and I are opposites. After sixteen years together, we are still opposites. He enjoys dinner with a few people, I enjoy big parties. He loves math and science and technology. I adore the arts. My husband is a rock solid, uneasily swayed man. I am a woman whose emotions resemble Mexican jumping beans flailing on a hot sidewalk.

We're different. Spaghetti and waffles. Venus and Mars. But we both have a desire, like the rest of humanity, to be loved. Completely and unconditionally. Our love for each other is imperfect, but because of God's perfect love given to us on the cross, we are called to love as He would.

This means not behaving rudely with each other and not seeking our own. Marriage is a like a laboratory for this kind of behavior. It takes years to find the perfect formula and along the way, explosions occur.

One huge help for us was reading the book *The Five Love Languages* by Gary Chapman. We learned that each of us *feel* loved through our own specific love language. Either 1) words of affirmation 2) gifts 3) service 4) time or 5) physical touch. John and I ascertained that my language is words of affirmation and his is service.

At the time we loved each other in the way that we felt love. So I loved John through words and he loved me through service. But I don't feel the most loved when I'm served. I feel it when John speaks kindness to me. And John doesn't receive love the most easily through words. He feels loved when I serve him. This was an epiphany for our marriage. In order to put aside rudeness and to not seek our own, we had to make a conscious decision to love each other using a specific love language.

Ergo, the microwave oven.

I can tell John he is wonderful over and over. I can give him gifts and spend time with him. All of which he enjoys. But when I decide to serve him, he lights up. I discovered that although he may never notice if I get my hair cut, wear something new or have a giant wart on my nose, he perks up when I clean out the microwave oven.

To me, it's a meaningless task. To John, it's a Hallmark card.

This makes no sense to me. At all.

But when does loving the opposite sex really make sense?

Today, focus on one person you love be it your spouse or child or friend. What is their love language? How can you love them in a way that will make them *feel* loved? It might not be what you think. It might even be a seemingly trivial act that sends the vital message of love.

Like cleaning out the microwave.

45 Family – Take It Up With God

"A time to weep, and a time to laugh; a time to mourn, and a time to dance." Ecclesiastes 3:4

John and I often look at our son and say, "Noah, we're your parents. Take it up with God."

I believe God uses all of life's circumstances to build our character and draw us closer to Him. So it is logical that He would use our families to mold us into what He wants. Sometimes that means He allows us to go through difficult times with family. We all know, to different degrees, how that feels.

But I also believe that God uses the joy of family. This past week Noah and I travelled to Baxter Springs, Kansas to visit my Aunt Carol Jo and Uncle Henry. We also got to spend time with my cousin Bert and his family. We toured Baxter Springs, which didn't take very long. We drove to Joplin, Missouri and ate and we took a stroll to Oklahoma. Uncle Henry spent some time teaching Noah about the Civil War history of Baxter Springs. My cousin Bert let Noah drive a tractor. Most of all, we visited and laughed. And I got to just *be* with my aunt whom I adore.

A wonderful time.

I have a "colorful" family. And I love the colors. My mom and dad were both raised in Texas, so many of my relatives have a southern twang when they speak. Add to that the language of many of my aunts and uncles and you get a unique group of folks. Profanity is used with the care of an artist's brush. Nothing blasphemous, just...colorful. Plus, they use idioms that I feel are gems like: "He's as worthless as spit in a puddle" or "Don't go having a squealing worm fit."

So visiting Carol Jo and Henry was a blast for me.

But I didn't choose to be in this family. I didn't ask to be in a family that makes me laugh so hard I cry or be in a family in which both my parents died before Noah was five. As that old saying goes we get to choose our friends but not our family.

God has taught me a lot through my family. Acceptance and honesty. Unconditional love. And of course, the joy of playing dominoes until late and visiting just for the sake of telling stories. I look at Noah and I hope he learns some good lessons from our family too. Time will tell.

Tonight, I was thinking about this Joyvotion and I asked Noah, "What is the best thing about our family, Noah?"

He answered, "The kindness. The love."

Surprised, I asked him, "Are you being serious?"

Quick as a flash he said, "No. It's the fact that we can afford video games."

I'm Noah's mom. I'll take it up with God.

46 You Got Him, God?

"'Do not be afraid of them, for I am with you and will rescue you,'
declares the Lord."
Jeremiah 1:8

Tonight was difficult. It was one of those times that I had to let go of control and once again whisper, "You got him, God?"

A few weeks ago I heard about Noah's school having a 6th grade party. Last week he said to me, "Mom, there's this dance." We were in the car and I almost veered into ongoing traffic. I told him I thought it was going to be a party. He informed me that a DJ would be there and that there'd be dancing.

"With girls?" I asked, trembling.

"I don't know." He humphed and changed the subject.

Tonight the party/dance took place at his middle school. I knew things were changing in my world as soon as he asked, "Mom, do I have any nice pants that are long enough?"

Thank God he said this when I was not operating heavy machinery.

We found appropriate clothes and he allowed me to comb his hair. As I combed, I wondered if hell was actually freezing over.

My neighbor and I decided to car pool. I delivered the two boys and my neighbor picked them up afterwards. When Noah's friend came down, Noah noticed his shoes, nice black ones.

"Mom, do I have any nice shoes?" We quickly tore apart his closet looking for the "nice shoes."

As I drove them, I had to open a window because my neighbor's son had apparently robbed a cologne store. But nothing prepared me for what happened next.

Noah had a tennis shoe on one foot and a nice black shoe on the other. He made a comment that the tennis shoe was more comfortable. Then he asked, "Brandon, which one looks better?"

Brandon answered, "Well, which one do you think *the ladies* would like?"

Again, angels protected us from having an accident. Noah's answer, "I don't know," pleased me. He went with the comfortable ones.

Once inside I told Noah I was going to go into the gym and check it out. He sternly told me that I had promised to leave. I told him I would after a peek.

As Noah joined a gaggle of guys, I surveyed the "party" area. I saw long tables of food and a giant dart board for nerf darts. Other games were scattered around but I didn't see a DJ anywhere. I sighed and contemplated breaking my promise to Noah. How could I leave my baby at a public school function at night? I'd thought about renting a drug sniffing dog, but I knew that would embarrass Noah. The gym was brightly lit and I checked everywhere for couches. None. And there were no bottles on the floor that they could spin.

So I left. And in the car, I prayed a prayer that has become one of my mother mantras: "God, you got him?"

"I got him." The Lord soothed my heart. This is not the first time I've uttered this prayer and it will not be the last. Noah will go off again and again into the world without me - as he should. But my Mama heart hurts, even as it laughs about the heavy cologne and talk of "the ladies." My faith in a God that cherishes and loves my boy more than I ever could comforts me.

And God had him. Noah came back tonight, a little sweaty and very happy. He informed me that he danced with a big group of his friends. No couples at all. And he had a blast.

"I danced every dance, Mom. Well, except for the one Justin Bieber song." He rolled his eyes.

God has our kids…and will always.

47 Get Out Of God's Way

"Oh, the depth of the riches of the wisdom and knowledge of God!
How unsearchable his judgments, and his paths beyond tracing out!"
Romans 11:33

Nine years ago, my husband and I talked about splitting up due to a wave of issues in our marriage. However, we decided to stick it out.

Two months after we decided to work through it, I saw little progress in John. He did not go to church as many times as I would want him to, he did not pray as I thought he should and he definitely didn't read the Bible as I told him. I knew the answers to all of our marital issues lay in pursuing Christ. I knew this and I told him and yet he refused.

One day I was praying for John using something akin to these words:

"Father, help John. He just isn't becoming the Spiritual leader that I know You want him to be. Help him, Lord, because he needs it. I have been trying to help him but he won't take it. Is there something else I should do?"

God answered my prayers. Immediately. With one simple phrase God told me exactly what I needed to do. He said, and I quote, "Robbie, Get Out of My Way!"

Ouch.

I started arguing with the Lord. Aren't I John's helpmate? Don't I have the responsibility to speak into His life?

And still all I heard, "Robbie, Get Out of My Way!"

I obeyed; I didn't talk to John about anything religious or spiritual for three months. This was extremely difficult for me. Whenever I wanted to say something to him, which was often, I prayed instead. Sometimes, those prayers were shouting and doubting prayers. Sometimes they were sighing and crying prayers. But then...

God and John developed this incredible intimacy that had nothing to do with me. My husband, who never had a relationship with his father, learned what it meant to have a Heavenly Father.

When we resumed our talks about God, it was a whole different ballgame. Instead of an arrogant lecturer, I became a partner with John in trying to figure out what God wanted for us to do. My husband became the spiritual leader.

Nine years later, I thank God for that horrible year of our marriage. God showed me that in trying to control my husband's spirituality, I was standing in the way of God working. It took me a long time to accept that my husband's relationship with Jesus does not look like my relationship with Jesus. The way he communicates with God does not include the Robbie-Six-Steps-To-Hanging-Out-With-Jesus plan.

So ladies, if you are wondering when your husband will ever become the spiritual leader you believe he should be, take a hard learned piece of wisdom: Get Out of God's Way. Pray harder than you've ever prayed, shouting and doubting, sighing and crying. And watch our Father do His thing in your man and in you!

48 Maybe, Maybe Not

"And we know that in all things God works for the GOOD of those who love Him, who have been called according to His purposes."
(NIV – Emphasis added) Romans 8:28

I love that I have a wise husband. He teaches me consistently about the Word of God. In fact the following Joyvotion is written by my man John.

Back in Genesis 3 (the fall of man) Adam and Eve ate from the Tree of the Knowledge of Good and Evil. Besides all the obvious consequences, (sin, death, and separation from God) I believe that tree had its own unique consequence for us all.

We "think" we are equipped to rightly judge good and evil. The problem is we lack the wisdom and perspective of God to know if something is truly good or evil.

I heard a story to illustrate the point. A poor farmer in a rural village had his only horse wander off and get lost. The people of the village came to lament the **evil** that had befallen the man. In response to them calling it **evil**, he said, "Maybe, maybe not." Days later the horse returned followed by six wild horses and the people of the village came to proclaim the **good** that had come to the man and he said, "Maybe, maybe not." Days later the man's only son was trying to train one of the horses and fell breaking his back leaving him paralyzed from the waist down. The people of the village came to lament the **evil** that had befallen the man and he said "Maybe, maybe not." Sometime after that the army came and drafted all the young men of the village except the man's son because he couldn't walk. Shortly after that news came that a battle resulted in the death of every young man from that village. The people of the village came to lament the **evil** that had befallen them all but the man said, "Maybe, maybe not."

Was this man wise beyond his years or did he simply understand he lacked the wisdom to judge good and evil rightly?

I am not arguing for a post-modern relativistic world view where everyone should pick the version of the truth that suits them. I am saying we judge all the time but lack the wisdom.

We live our lives judging people, places and circumstances as good or evil based on the simple criteria: Does this benefit me or not? As followers of Christ, we may extend the criteria of our judgment to include God's Will as we understand it that day, but it is still our judgment.

Ten or twenty years ago, I would have believed that the greatest **evil** affecting my life was my addiction. Today I am convinced that in God's hands it was and is the greatest **good** because apart from that pain, I would never have fully bent my knee to the Lord and been set free by His love and grace. Clearly I was wrong before and it is not completely clear that I am right now.

The next time you find yourself judging I hope you can let go of your right to judge and instead trust God to be the only Righteous Judge. Is this circumstance good? Is it evil?

Maybe, maybe not.

49 Discount Dog Gamble

"But God demonstrates His own love for us in this:
While we were still sinners, Christ died for us." Romans 5:8

We huddled in a small room, our eyes focused on a Chug, or a Pug Chihuahua. The pet store clerk came and I began asking questions, believing that the answers would tell me the idea of taking this pooch home was silly.

The Chug was skinny and sick with Kennel Cough, Giardia and maybe more. He had been in the store for three months and had been rejected time after time. The clerk took home his sister but couldn't take him.

"Maybe he needs us." I said, and looked at John who was obviously ready to drop this spontaneous idea and go home.

John, Noah and I talked it over. This would be a gamble. The little guy might not make it.

But I knew I wanted him. "John, he is on sale." And then I played the ultimate wife card. "Honey, this could be my birthday present."

A while later we were at the counter with another couple, also getting a puppy. Their dog looked perfect and cost $1200. Ours, a little sick thing, cost *much* less. But Noah and I were thrilled as we carried our new little five-month-old puppy to the car.

"What should we name him?" I asked.

"He looks like a Thor." John said, kidding. But it stuck. Thor Reginald Iobst became our fifth family member.

Buyer's remorse came quickly as I stayed up most of the night listening to this six pound baby hack every thirty minutes as if he'd been smoking three packs a day for years. He promptly pooped and peed everywhere but wouldn't eat.

We took him to the vet and she prescribed him medicine, paid for by the pet store, and told us the beginnings of pneumonia were in his lungs. But there was hope.

As I've prayed for Thor, I've contemplated the value of life. And I've experienced gratitude.

We are all sick in our sin and desperately need someone who will take a chance on us. God stepped in and paid the ultimate price, Jesus' life, to save us from a life of being caged in and rejected. Even if we poop and pee through life, making messes of our lives, He comes in and cleans up and holds us.

At first I didn't want fall in love with Thor. What if he died? But as I've watched him go from a hacking puppy to a scampering dog, his paws have scooted their way into my heart.

How much more does the Father cherish each of us?

We rescued Thor and I'm glad. Scooby, our Puggle, isn't. He looks at the new puppy as a nuisance in his life, like a fly that won't go away. He will stare at us and I know he's thinking, "Wasn't I enough?"

But in rescuing Thor, I have been given the gift of experiencing a tiny iota of what God might feel when He looks at us.

Unconditional love.

50 I'm A Horrible Mother!

"Grace and peace to you, from God our Father."
Colossians 1:2

John Wooden, the late record-setting basketball coach of UCLA, defined success as *peace of mind that is the direct result of self-satisfaction in knowing you did your best to become the best that you are capable of becoming.*

So what is it to be a successful mom?

This morning, my son Noah, who has asthma and has had pneumonia for the past few days, was able to go to school. In the silence of my home, I began to beat myself up.

If I was a good mom, he would not be sick so often.

If I was a good mom, Noah would have a clean home all the time.

If I was a good mom, I wouldn't have gotten a second dog.

If I was a good mom, I would feed him only organics and eliminate the junk and never get angry and only show him Jesus' love!

But I'm not and I don't.

This afternoon I met with my Moms in Touch group. We pray for our kids at school. When asked what my prayer request was for my son, I burst out into tears. "I'm a horrible mother!"

I made a bit of a scene.

My friends did not coddle me, but instead told me truth that I needed to hear: There is a difference between being a perfect mom and a successful mom. One of them quoted Wooden.

John Wooden also said that in order to be successful, I must be the best ME I can be. So to be a successful mom, I need to be the best I can be...in *my* talents and *my* deficiencies.

My parents taught me to respect God, laugh at life and be friendly. But they didn't teach me much about money. In fact, I've had problems in that area. If John were writing this, he'd type, "Amen!"

Were my parents' successful? Yes! As my dad often said, "We do the best we can."

I want to be the mom that Noah needs. For me, that means accepting that I am not a clean freak, I allow him to have fast food and I can use words that are simply idiotic. It means realizing that I can get better in these areas, but I don't need to beat myself up when he gets sick.

It means living out the Serenity Prayer by Reinhold Niebuhr:

God, give me the serenity to accept the things I cannot change, (Noah's health)

The courage to change the things I can, (The things that God tells me to change)

and the wisdom to know the difference. (And not beat myself up.)

Am I a good mom? A successful mom? Not always.

But I have peace of mind that today I have done my best to become the best mom I can be.

That is God's grace. And that is enough.

꧁

51 Stick The Landing!

"Humble yourselves, therefore, under God's mighty hand..."
1 Peter 5:6

My favorite event in the Olympics is Women's Gymnastics. If I'd been born with another body, a desire to work for hours in a gym and a love for balance beams and vaults, well...I'd be a gold medalist.

But alas, the only Olympic sport I have any knack for is mothering. Oh, that's not in the Olympics? It should be.

My 13-year-old boy is a joy to my heart and I love him more than my own life.

YET, many, okay *most* days I don't make it to the medal ceremony or even past the quarterfinals. It's difficult to stick the landing in parenting.

For example, last Saturday a battle occurred in the Iobst home. Noah disobeyed me. In gold medal fashion, I talked to him about it in a normal tone and doled out appropriate discipline. I then asked him to do three tasks for me while I went to the store. I came back to find disobedience run rampant.

One of the number one rules of training to be a mom, especially of a teenager, is to never take disobedient behavior personally. He is 13. He's a great kid but he's absent-minded and much more concerned about his own existence than mine. Ergo, he's 13.

I ignored the rule. He made these choices to inflict pain upon me and how dare he not be concerned about my life and my heart??!!! I became furious and broke rule number two:

Never discipline in anger.

I did. The battle raged. Voices were raised, doors were slammed, and dogs ran into corners, scared for their own lives.

I blew it. No medal. Not even a trip to London.

The rest of the day we were civil, but pouty. Yes, both of us.

In church the next day John sat between us, continuing to shake his head metaphorically at the war of emotions he'd come home to Saturday night.

The pastor spoke about communion. God spoke to me about my heart and the grace He had for me…and Noah. Humbled, I knew what I had to do.

"Noah, please forgive me for my anger yesterday. I love you. Mom."

I passed the note to Noah, breaking a lesser known rule of mothering: Don't pass notes in church.

He read it, looked at me and grinned. His note came back:

"K. LOL. You should forgive me. I'm sorry."

The National Anthem started playing and I went to the gold medal spot, accompanied by my son.

It's difficult to stick the landing as a parent, but allowing humility and forgiveness to be part of the daily routine always results in a winning score.

52 When Fear Rings Your Door Bell

"He (the Priest) shall say: 'Hear, Israel: Today you are going into battle against your enemies. Do not be fainthearted or afraid; do not panic or be terrified by them. For the Lord your God is the one who goes with you to fight for you against your enemies to give you victory.'"
Deuteronomy 20:3-4

Like Professor Moriarty to Sherlock Holmes, Wyle Coyote to the Roadrunner and yes, the Joker to Batman, FEAR has been my nemesis all of my life.

I've fought hard against it using Scripture and prayer, practical mind diversion techniques and even therapy. Today I can say I am a courageous woman who lives in freedom, only because of the way the Lord has fought for me against my enemy.

And then…

A deranged man, full of evil, enters a theater 25 minutes from my house and kills 12 people and injures 58 others.

My family is safe. My nephew went to one of the other theaters in Aurora for a midnight showing of Batman and came home happy and unharmed.

We all were bombarded with the tragic news the next morning. I was out drinking coffee on my balcony when a neighbor walked by and said, "Turn your TV on, Robbie and pray."

Fear rang the door bell as I sat and watched the news. I let him in and he sat with me as my heart broke for those parents and family members of those shot. I cried and shook my head at the senselessness of such an EVIL act.

That day Noah was scheduled to go to Water World with some friends. Fear whispered to me, "Don't let him go. Who knows what could happen at an amusement park today."

The old battle raged. Do I try to control the future by gripping my son with white knuckles? Do I keep him close so I can run interference for any danger? If I don't, what if something happens to him? What if I get a call like those precious family members of the 12 in Aurora? What if the worst possible event happens?

The door bell rang again. I answered and there stood Faith. I let him in. He whispered to me, "God is in control, Robbie. You are not. God adores you and John and Noah. The enemy does not."

Decision time. I bowed my head and prayed for the courage to be courageous. God's strength filled me and I told Fear to get the hell out of my home and go to hell!!

He left. I cried some more and Faith helped wipe my tears. I surrendered AGAIN my life and my son's life to God. "You got Him today, right, Lord?"

"Yes, I do."

Not a promise that something horrible won't happen. Not assurance that I won't be faced with indescribable pain at some point. But PEACE, a lovely blanket that covers me with the joy of not having to spend time wondering and worrying and fretting. Peace that passes understanding.

No matter where you are in the world, when such evil runs rampant, you are affected by fear. Could that ever happen to me or my loved ones?

Dear friend, I encourage you to kick fear out of your home in the name of Jesus and let Faith hang out on your couch with you.

Join me and let's keep walking with His courage one step at a time, no matter what the enemy does! Our Mighty God fights for us! As we let Him do battle, His JOY fills our homes and our families!

About The Author

Robbie Iobst is an award-winning speaker and author. Her stories have been seen in several compilation books including eight *Chicken Soup for the Soul* titles. Through Robbie's love for Jesus and infectious humor, she encourages others to courageously follow Christ. Robbie lives in Centennial, Colorado with husband John, son Noah and dogs Scooby and Thor. If you would like to receive Robbie's free Joy-votions in your email each week, let her know at robbieiobst@hotmail.com. Get to know Robbie at her blog www.robbieiobst.blogspot.com or her website www.robbieiobst.com

www.ingramcontent.com/pod-product-compliance
Lightning Source LLC
Chambersburg PA
CBHW072024040426
42447CB00009B/1716